Flower Color Theory

Flower Color Theory

Taylor and Michael Putnam

Introduction

Our first book, *Flower Color Guide,* introduced readers
to flower selection and seasonality. It would have
been incredibly helpful when we started our business,
Putnam & Putnam, in 2014 in New York City. Our next
learning was actualizing color theory, and what we have
discovered, we share here in our second book.

When arranging, we first think about color; naturally, we
wanted to create a complete guide on how we use color.
As it always has, color inspires our work. Color is the path
in flower arranging. It seeds composition, to continue the
gardening metaphor. *Flower Color Theory* brings readers
to the next level, offering lessons on how to combine and
use the flowers that you now know to create stunning
arrangements.

   We've been in the midst of some very dark days lately.
Especially in cities, flowers have been hard to come by.
We had just finished photographing the images in this
book a few weeks earlier when the flower market in New
York City closed, and we, along with the rest of the city,
quarantined. These photographs of our arrangements are
links to happier times.

   We have noticed in our travels around the world,
teaching workshops about flower arranging, that the
countries most challenged economically seem to often
be painted in the brightest colors—vibrant and wild.
One thinks of India, for instance, with its vivid saris and
animals adorned with flowers and other decorations.

   Wherever you are, appreciating color can transform
and improve your experience of living. Working with
flowers is a great way to learn how to value color, and

this book will teach you how to do exactly that by showing you how to use color.

If you are intimidated by color, don't be. Color is energy. It's feeling and emotion. If you walk into a room, you're going to feel completely different if the room is painted red or if it's painted yellow.

When we teach workshops or consult with new clients, we always ask them to leave any assumptions about color at the door, from the onset. Likewise, we ask you to go deeper into how color can make a statement—your statement, not a culturally mandated cliché. Use color however you want, whenever and wherever you want to express any emotion you want to evoke. Just like people, flowers can be nonbinary and fluid. When a client wants an arrangement "for a man" and asks for it to be "very masculine," we just smile and tell them to buy their buddy a plant.

We think about flowers in an emotional way rather than merely decoratively. When you arrange flowers, start by deciding what it is that you want to say with them. What is the occasion? Is it a romantic dinner for two or a night of self-care, just you at home? Is it a birthday party? A wedding shower? What's the vibe you want to create? A happy holiday? A dance party? Something sexy? Reverential?

Black, obviously, is morose—although it can also be very sophisticated. One of our fantasies is to do a wedding with all black, meaning dark, flowers. It would be so elegant.

Blue is serene. Red is passion. But red is also polarizing because of its association with Christmas, Valentine's Day, and Chinese New Year. Sometimes, the best use of red is as an accent in the gradation of other colors. We love red, that rich orangey red that is associated with Baroque elegance and abundance. It's the color that's so prominent in Dutch still life paintings. It pulls out all the decadent energy in these masterpieces.

Following a color scheme can help you decide where to take your arrangement. In this book, our arrangements are built around a variety of color schemes: Accent Color, Analogous, Complementary, Monochromatic, Rainbow, Transitional, and Triadic. These specific color schemes can help set the overall tone of your arrangement. For example, a monochromatic palette, which uses a single hue in different shades, can be tame and simple, whereas a triadic palette, which pulls color from three equidistant points on the color wheel, creates energy and noise. See pages 14 and 372 to learn more about these schemes. Let these groupings help guide you when choosing your colors.

Once you've established the emotional tone and color direction, move on to the specific elements. We think of flowers like actors in a play. There are the lead players and the supporting actors, and then there are the bit players who can sometimes steal the show. Like actors, flowers come in all types, but there are four essential groups: face flowers, fillers, textural flowers, and gestural stems. Face flowers are your showstoppers—the biggest blooms in your arrangement. Filler flowers come next, as your base, a sort of canvas on which to place other flowers. Textural elements add visual interest and gestural stems add movement, creating the illusion of dancing flowers.

See what's available from your florist or at your farm stand or, if you're lucky, in your own garden. You don't have to spend a fortune. Welcome daisies and carnations into your home. In this book, you will see different styles of flower arranging, using flowers, first and foremost, but also fruit, vegetables, and the like. Any of the many beautiful things that flower on the Earth can add texture and interest to your arrangements. If you live somewhere where flowers aren't easily available or are cost-prohibitive, perhaps you can find some nice brown pears and use some of the pretty pink tulips you may have planted. You can make something beautiful from simple elements.

When you start arranging, assign principle roles to two stems that represent different sides of the color spectrum and then build on those using color. Add more stems of different tones and shades, focusing on the in-between. This skill, like any other, will become instinctive with time and practice. You will develop an appreciation for color that is both sophisticated and emotional. Monochromatic arrangements, surprisingly, can also be designed this way. Monochromatic flowers are never fully monochrome because all flowers have so much color in them, and they can be used to shape arrangements that are incredibly graphic and textured.

When we design, our goal is to gradate colors and avoid what we call the polka-dot school of flower arranging. Instead, we focus attention on all the colors in between the two flowers at either end of the color spectrum of the arrangement. Think of the spectrum as a kind of rainbow that flows from left to right, top to bottom.

You should always look for the properties of the colors you are arranging with. There is the tint, when a color is mixed with white so that the color goes lighter. There is shade, when a color is mixed with black, increasing darkness. Tone results from mixing a color with gray, or by both tinting and shading.

The way you see color will always inform the way you express and share your feelings, in a style distinctively your own. If you want to create an arrangement that's soft and ethereal, focus on transition, a soft gradation from one color to another. Whether it's a cool color or a warm color, or even two warm colors, doesn't matter. If you want an energetic arrangement, then create contrast. Instead of all-gradated transition, make it pop with a sharp accent. Maybe it's a shot of red or sharp yellow or orange that will energize the design. A flower you use to punctuate an arrangement is one that breaks up any visual monotony, whereas flowers that accent an arrangement complement the overall palette.

Most importantly, find inspiration in unexpected sources—people, places, objects—and keep them in mind for the final product. Our ikebana homage to the art of Japanese flower arranging was inspired by the desire to create harmony between the flowers and their containers. There are also many romantic and formal arrangements in the book, which were inspired by our appreciation of art, architecture, and travel. What you won't see here are flowers in dome-shaped arrangements. We like to stay away from the unnatural. They are, in our estimation, 1990s clichés. Flowers don't gather in dome shapes.

Can you train your eye to see color in more depth? Squint your eyes so they're almost closed and look at a flower arrangement. What do you see? You don't see the details of the arrangement, but you see the colors and you feel the emotion that it elicits.

While we were creating the arrangements for this book, we frequently visited museums for inspiration. We went to the Guggenheim Museum and the Museum of Modern

Art in New York City and the Clark Art Institute in Williamstown, Massachusetts. We wanted to see how the artists we admired used color. If you squint when you look at a work, the noise is canceled out a little bit and you're able to see color as a block, as a field. In cases when we thought that we could do a really cool arrangement with a block of color, we'd take a photograph of the painting. Michael would do a quick visual sketch, and from there, we would come up with the color swatches that we would use when we went to the flower market. That step in the process is the inspiration for the color swatches in the back of this book.

How you look at flowers says a lot about how you look at life. "There are always flowers for people who want to see them," said Henri Matisse. And Georgia O'Keeffe was offended when people ignored the profound beauty of flowers. She decided that if she could paint a flower on a huge scale, which she did, "you could not ignore its beauty," she explained.

In our workshops, we always say that what we are doing is painting—that flowers are our medium and color is the message.

Smell the roses—smell all the flowers, we've been told. Our advice is to see their colors.

How to use this book

Use this book as both a guide and a source for inspiration. You'll learn how to combine color and be motivated to use color in unexpected ways. Inside, you'll find 175 arrangements in color palettes that represent nearly the entire spectrum of colors occurring in flowers.

Use the captions to identify the primary color scheme, the most prominent colors, and the elements, such as the flowers, foliage, or fruit, of the arrangement. For the elements, we listed the main ingredients—the elements which we see as most outstanding—using their common names. These names, we realize, can differ around the world, so we included those that we most often use in New York City. If you'd like, you can refer to our first book for the botanical names. We've also included a takeaway for each design. Think of these as tips for creating your own arrangement at home. Along the side of the page, you'll see a bar with the arrangement's color palette. Of course, we know you that you may need to make substitutions, as the colors may vary based on the season and availability. We've included corresponding, removable swatches in the back of the book. Take them to your local flower market when shopping for your own arrangements.

For this book, understanding the color schemes is important. Each arrangement is categorized as one of the following: Accent Color, Analogous, Complementary, Monochromatic, Rainbow, Transitional, or Triadic. We've defined them on the following page, but for more information on basic color theory and how to apply it when arranging, see the appendix on page 371.

Key Color Schemes

Accent Color   is color used for emphasis.

Analogous   is a group of three to four colors next to each other on the color wheel. We like to think outside the box—or wheel—for this scheme, and often use neutrals to connect colors within the design. Incorporate neutrals, such as cream, gray, or white, with undertones of the analogous colors to help blend the overall palette.

Complementary   is two colors directly opposite each other on the color wheel.

Monochromatic   is a single base hue.

Rainbow   is the use of all colors on the color wheel.

Transitional   is the gradual movement from one color to the next.

Triadic   is a group of three colors evenly spaced out on the color wheel.

Caption

List of elements (we've identified the primary elements using their common name)

Color scheme

Accent Color
White and cream with
mauve accent

Ranunculus, Snake's head
fritillary, Sweet pea

Using a subtle checkerboard
pattern—as this snake's head
fritillary does—makes the
arrangement of white florals pop.

Key colors in the
arrangement

Tip or takeaway

Arrangements

Black and White

Tulip, Ranunculus, Anemone,
Scabiosa, Sweet pea, Blackberry,
Privet berry

Shape and hard lines, such as
the dramatic band of black florals
running through the arrangement,
bring interest and depth to a
black-and-white design.

Accent Color
White and cream with mauve accent

Ranunculus, Snake's head fritillary, Sweet pea

Using a subtle checkerboard pattern—as this snake's head fritillary does—makes the arrangement of white florals pop.

Analogous
Silver, gray, and white

Dusty miller, Paper white,
Silver-painted fern, Lichen-
covered branch

Use barren branches to create
a hauntingly beautiful silhouette,
perfect for the winter months.

Accent Color
White with green accent

Phalaenopsis orchid, Sweet pea,
Olive, Wax flower

Olive branches are a versatile
base available year-round.
The soft green pairs beautifully
with whites and neutrals.

Accent Color
White and cream with pale green accent

Hellebore, Ranunculus, Daffodil, Tulip, Thunberg spirea

The green of the hellebore works as an accent color here. Always consider the center of florals as a part of the color palette.

Monochromatic
White

Ranunculus, Dutch iris, Bleeding heart, Chamomile, Allium

Monochromatic arrangements offer creative freedom. By focusing less on color combinations, you can place emphasis on shape.

Complementary
Yellow and purple

Sweet pea, Tulip, Pansy,
Ranunculus, Thunberg spirea

The geometry of color blocking brings a modern touch to romantic arrangements. Here, the hint of yellow in the white pansies allows for a softer color block.

Accent Color
Black and white with
silver-green and lilac accents

Tulip, Calla lily, Kalanchoe pumila

Calla lily and tulip stems
are incredibly malleable and
relatively difficult to break,
allowing you to manipulate them
for more gestural expression.

Analogous
Gray, silver green, and white

Begonia, Ranunculus, Rose, Sweet pea, Paper white

Place large begonia leaves—always a great backdrop for soft white flowers—at the center of a design.

Analogous
Silver green, cream, and mauve

Hellebore, Silver spear

Make an impact with only two elements by manipulating the foliage into sculptural forms.

Analogous
Silver green, gray, and white

Lichen-covered branch, Calla lily

To create a minimalist design,
let one element inspire the
shape, like these lichen-covered
branches, and build off it.

Accent Color
White with pale blue
and yellow accents

Cecropia leaf, Daffodil, Muscari,
Ranunculus, Pansy, Pussy willow,
Thunberg spirea

Using a wide, light-colored
element, such as these leaves,
as the background allows the
flowers to show off their shape
and color.

Analogous
White, purple, mauve,
and pink

Cecropia leaf, Rose, Snake
allium, Ranunculus, Thunberg
spirea, Kale

Wider designs allow for the
presence of negative space at
the center of the arrangement.
Use this space to spotlight
delicate, gestural stems.

Analogous
Gray, silver green,
and pale blue

Limonium, Dusty miller,
Tweedia, Kalanchoe

Binding clusters of elements,
such as Limonium, with wire
will control the shape and
gesture of any unruly actors
in your arrangements.

Accent Color
Silver green with mauve accent

Rose, Ranunculus, Limonium, Kalanchoe pumila, Thunberg spirea, Muscari, Dusty miller, Bergenia, Poppy pod

When accenting with a warm color, use a silver-green base as a softer alternative to white.

Analogous
Mauve, cream, and white

Hellebore, Ranunculus, Snake allium, Slender velvet bush

Use gestural elements, like snake allium, to form a border around other florals, creating a design that is wild yet contained.

Accent Color
Beige, plum, and black with apricot accent

Cymbidium orchid, Cantaloupe, Ranunculus, Sweet pea, Rose, Calla lily, Privet berry

Color blocking allows for multiple points of emphasis. The inclusion of large fruit, such as the cantaloupe here, is an easy way to create a brilliant concentration of color.

Analogous
Brown, peach, and beige

Phalaenopsis orchid, Wheat,
Variegated New Zealand flax leaf

Minimalist arrangements can be
just as impactful as lush designs.
Focus emphasis on a single line
or gesture.

Transitional
From gold to white

Phalaenopsis orchid, Painted cypress, Sweet pea

Break away from traditional use of red or green for winter holiday arrangements. Metallic gold and white can be just as festive and are more versatile.

Complementary
Beige and lavender

Carnation, Sweet pea, Muscari, Tweedia, Dried grass

Gather together florals with similar attributes. Concentrations of like flowers result in an arrangement with a more natural look.

Monochromatic
Beige

Rose, Sweet pea, Lisianthus,
Wax flower, Wheat

Having no associations with a
specific holiday or special event,
beige is a neutral color, perfect
for any time of the year.

Transitional
Apricot, cream, butter yellow, and chartreuse

Rose, Tulip, Ranunculus, Corkscrew hazel, Fig, Eucalyptus, Daisy

Use figs for punctuation in lighter-hued designs. When cut open, they reveal apricot, brown, and pink tones that meld well with the color scheme.

Accent Color
Beige, yellow, and brown with
sienna accent

Goldenrod, Eucalyptus, Rose,
Phalaenopsis orchid, Wax flower,
Western red cedar

Consider the color of stems
as part of the overall palette.
The goldenrod and eucalyptus
stems here add an earthy tone
to the composition.

Monochromatic
Blush

Tulip, Rose, Sweet pea,
Lisianthus, Nerine

Sweet pea, with its soft color
and texture, adds a delicate
touch that brings a romantic
look to arrangements.

Accent Color
Pink and blush with silver accent

Rose, Anthurium, Dusty miller, Japanese quince, Silver-painted fern

A silver metallic accent always gives a composition a ceremonious and theatrical look.

Accent Color
Blush with scarlet accent

Rose, Lisianthus, Tulip, Rhubarb, Sweet pea

Find a way to move color throughout an arrangement. The red of the rhubarb directs the eye from the red roses to the rest of the composition.

Accent Color
Peach, cream, and blush with
dusty rose accent

Rose, Tulip, Hellebore, Olive,
Sweet pea, Cathedral bells,
Thunberg spirea, Fig

Olive branches are a wonderful
alternative to pure green foliage
to soften a palette. The silver
undertones work beautifully with
the warm hues.

Transitional With Accent
From pink to cream with
blue accent

Tulip, Ranunculus, Rose,
Thunberg spirea, Sweet pea,
Stock, Muscari

Add an accent color to the
lighter-toned side of an
arrangement. It balances out
the overall design, increasing
its impact.

Transitional
From blush to pale blue

Rose, Sweet pea, Larkspur, Ranunculus, Lisianthus, Clematis, Nerine

The use of glass vases offers transparency, making stems important players in the arrangement. Use the deeper-hued stems to create a stark contrast to the pastel petals.

Accent Color
Pink with pale blue
and black accents

Rose, Sweet pea, Muscari,
Lavender, Eucalyptus,
Philodendron 'Imperial Red',
Fringed lavender

Add a dark dash of color to a
bright pastel palette to inject
intensity to the arrangement.

Accent Color
Blush, peach, and cream with
purple accent

Poppy, Rose, Anemone, Tulip,
Sweet pea, Flowering cherry

When working with two vessels,
create continuity in the shape
of the arrangements. This helps
pull them together, making a
single vignette.

Accent Color
Blush and pink with black accent

Philodendron 'Imperial Red', Tulip, Ranunculus, Rose, Plum blossom

Florals with a wide face, like the philodendron, can act as the base structure and showcase the other elements in the arrangement.

Monochromatic
Pink

Peony, Rose, Ranunculus,
Corkscrew willow, Amaranth,
Strawflower, Emerald ripple
peperomia, Lisianthus

To create a horizontal composition
with vertical vessels, keep florals
low and wide, incorporating
cascading elements, such as
amaranth and corkscrew willow.

Analogous
Cream, pink, and blush

Tulip, Bromeliad, Rose,
Ranunculus, Sweet pea,
Carnation, Calathea leaf

Pair spring flowers with warm-
climate elements, such as
bromeliads, for a tropical feeling.

Analogous
Pink, peach, and apricot

Peony, Ranunculus, Sweet pea, Rose, Bleeding heart, Chamomile, Daffodil, Thunberg spirea

Bright pastels, like peach and apricot, are cheerful and uplifting. As analogous colors, this combination ensures a seamless appearance.

Transitional
From butter yellow to pink

Poinsettia, Rose, Anthurium,
Japanese quince, Tulip,
Hellebore, Ranunculus, Daisy

A poinsettia can be used as
both a base foliage and a focal
element. The colorful leaves,
with hints of pink and yellow,
unite the composition.

Analogous
Pink, blush, cream, peach,
and yellow

Poppy, Tulip, Hellebore,
Snake's head fritillary, Daffodil,
Sweet pea

Using florals of a similar tone
heightens the seamlessness
of an analogous design and is
gentler on the eye.

Complementary
Peach and pale blue

Carnation

When creating a composition
with only one type of flower,
focus on color variation
and the desired shape of
the arrangement.

Accent Color
Orange, brown, and peach
with burgundy accent

Crown imperial fritillary, Tulip,
Blood orange, Ranunculus,
Eucalyptus, Pussy willow

Employing vessels made of
different materials, like glass
and ceramic here, adds texture
to a composition.

Complementary
Peach and pale blue

Tulip, Ranunculus, Daffodil, Muscari, Sweet pea, Statice, Rose

Add blue to arrangements with warm colors. Inspired by old Flemish paintings, this design features a touch of contrast with the blue Muscari, making the other florals pop.

Transitional
From chartreuse to beige

Rose, Lady's slipper orchid, Ivy, Lisianthus, Sweet pea, Western red cedar, Wheat

A loose, textural, rambling element, like ivy, always evokes a certain English-garden feeling.

Complementary
Peach and chartreuse

Ginger, Coconut, Anthurium,
Grass, Poppy, Goldenrod,
Palm nut

This arrangement works because
of its strong use of texture.
Each element is unique in
character, but the components
come together beautifully to
create a cohesive design.

Analogous With Accent
Peach, yellow green, and
pale blue with purple accent

Poppy, Anemone, Muscari,
Anthurium, Sweet pea

Adding a dark punctuation to a
simple arrangement immediately
makes it more interesting and
dynamic. Here, a purple accent
within the light analogous palette
creates energy.

Accent Color
Yellow and pale green with pink accent

Plum blossom, Forsythia, Grapes, Tulip, Daffodil, Rose, Lemon

Incorporate several varieties of flowering branches, such as plum blossom and forsythia, in a single composition to add strong lines of energy to the arrangement.

Monochromatic
Dusty purple

Dutch iris, Lilac, Rose, Lupine

In a monochromatic design, staggering the heights of the elements helps create vertical movement and depth.

Accent Color
Lavender with cream accent

Asparagus, Sweet pea, Clematis

Give people something to talk about by inserting unusual produce, like cream-colored asparagus, into your design.

Accent Color
Lavender with coral accent

Stock, Sweet pea, Rose, Tulip, Limonium, Kalanchoe pumila

Long linear swaths of color always break up a monochromatic palette, sending the eye in pleasing directions.

Accent Color
Pale blue and blue with
blush accent

Rose, Muscari, Larkspur, Globe
allium, Sweet pea

Find inspiration in unexpected
places—or people. Inspired
by Marie Antoinette, this
arrangement incorporates her
penchant for pale blue and blush
and evokes a French court.

Analogous
Pale blue, blue, and purple

Muscari, Larkspur, Love-in-a-mist, Anemone

Color-block florals in simple arrangements to make them appear more dynamic.

Analogous
White, yellow, and green

Daffodil, Ranunculus, Variegated
Japanese silver grass

For a purposefully untamed look,
manipulate the grass to encircle
the florals, encaging them within
its blades.

Monochromatic
Pale green

Lisianthus, Lady's slipper orchid,
Carnation, Cymbidium orchid,
Cypress branch

For an arrangement with a bright
and youthful energy, introduce
pale green.

Accent Color
Chartreuse, pale green, and
orange with yellow-orange accent

Lady's slipper orchid,
Lisianthus, Daffodil, Orange,
Cymbidium orchid, Eucalyptus
pod, Ivy

Household vessels, such as
pitchers and mugs, offer an
effortless and rustic look.

Accent Color
Pale green and chartreuse
with purple accent

Vanda orchid, Sweet pea, Poppy,
Grapes, Palm nut, Pepperberry

Be creative with how you
incorporate green elements.
Rather than using only foliage,
try grapes or palm nuts for an
added punch.

Accent Color
Green, pale green,
and chartreuse with pale
blue accent

Calathea leaf, Larkspur, Globe
allium, Chrysanthemum, Coconut,
Goldenrod, Globe artichoke,
Grapes, Muscari

Use the patterns within nature
as a tool. The marbled, sharp
lines of the foliage juxtaposed
with the soft colors of the florals
create vibrancy.

Complementary
Pale green and blush

Poppy, Sweet pea, Hellebore,
Fern, Palm nut, Bergenia

Incorporating elements that offer
movement will make a simple
arrangement more impactful.

Monochromatic
Butter yellow

Peony, Rose, Tulip, Ranunculus,
Passion vine, Dumb cane leaf,
Queen Anne's lace, Daffodil bulb

Here, a vine weaves in a circular
path around the entirety of
the composition and between the
dissimilar vessels, making them
feel like one.

Accent Color
Butter yellow with dark
green accent

Rose, Hellebore, Tulip, Cavolo
nero kale, Ranunculus, Fern

A backdrop of dark foliage
contrasts with lighter-hued
florals, showcasing the flowers
and emphasizing their beauty.

Accent Color
Green with white accent

Peppergrass, Iris, Bleeding heart

Make movement the focus of an arrangement. Here, the sinuous gestural lines of the expressive peppergrass add allure.

Analogous
White, cream, and brown

Ranunculus, Daffodil, Hellebore, Dwarf crown imperial fritillary, Eucalyptus

Break up green florals with touches of brown. Acting as a patina, it gives the arrangement the look of an Old World painting.

Analogous
Peach, cream, and apricot

Palm, Anthurium, Rose, Daffodil

A floral frog has only so much real estate. Focus on adding strong individual elements rather than clustering a handful of florals.

Monochromatic
Green

Begonia, Pallid fritillary,
Huckleberry, Fern, Rosemary

To add depth to any
monochromatic arrangement,
mix up the color's tones, as seen
here with the range of greens.

Accent Color
White with silver-green accent

Palm, Daffodil, Ranunculus, Thunberg spirea, Sweet pea, Tulip

To help white florals pop, arrange them in front of large, graphic leaves, such as palm fronds.

Accent Color
Pale green and green with
plum accent

Hellebore, Dwarf crown imperial
fritillary, Fig, Tulip, Privet berry,
Paper white

Break up bright colors in an
arrangement by using black and
plum as punctuation points.

Accent Color
White and black with
brown accent

Protea, Calla lily, Pampas grass,
Ranunculus, Muscari, Snake's
head fritillary

When you substitute grass in
place of branches, it adds an
additional layer of texture and
sets the shape of an entire
arrangement, as seen here.

Monochromatic
Green

Alocasia, Pitcher plant, Lady's slipper orchid, Fern, Grass, String of pearls

A composition made almost exclusively of foliage is just as impactful as one of flowers. Employ leaves with interesting colors and patterns for variety.

Analogous
Green, pale green, chartreuse, and butter yellow

Poppy, Begonia, Daffodil, Fragrant sumac

Here, the shape of the poppies mimics the spots on the begonia, gathering the elements together.

Accent Color
Silver with orange accent

Heliconia, Eucalyptus,
Dusty miller, Persimmon,
Papaya, Juniper, Grapes, Rose

It's acceptable to create
arrangements with or without
just one type of flower. Here,
the focus is on the foliage, with
the heliconia floral serving as
a pop of color.

Accent Color
Chartreuse and ocher with
butter yellow accent

Anthurium, Rose, Sweet pea,
Tulip, Thunberg spirea

Incorporate elements with
like colors. The ocher in the
anthurium mirrors the ocher
of the sweet pea, unifying
the color palette.

Monochromatic
Chartreuse

Anthurium, Lady's slipper orchid,
Cymbidium orchid, Vanda orchid,
Porcini mushroom, Asparagus,
Palm nut

Mushrooms or other fungi can
be an unexpected element in
a composition. They come in a
variety of colors, such as white,
red, and yellow, and can work
in nearly any design.

Accent Color
Chartreuse and pale green
with plum accent

Anthurium, Amaryllis, Lady's
slipper orchid, Cymbidium
orchid, Calla lily, Scabiosa,
Ranunculus, Grapes, Palm nut,
Blackberry

When possible, source handmade
glass vessels. The material has
more warmth than their mass-
produced counterparts, and its
imperfections can add a unique
element to a composition.

Complementary
Plum and yellow

Poppy, Forsythia, Persian fritillary, Dutch iris, Daffodil

To evoke the relaxed feel of a spring garden, group iris and forsythia together.

Accent Color
Plum, sienna, and silver green
with yellow accent

Strawflower, Begonia, Lisianthus,
Persian fritillary, Sweet pea,
Kangaroo paw, Goldenrod,
Eucalyptus

Accent colors do not need to
be concentrated in a single
area. Here, the yellow florals are
sprinkled throughout to allow
your attention to travel within
the design.

Accent Color
Burgundy and blush with
chartreuse accent

Anthurium, Ranunculus, Rose,
Sweet pea, Tulip, Cherry
blossom, Palm nut, Pepperberry

Position concentrations of color
in overlapping lines, creating a
focal point where the two colors
cross. The result is a bold and
impactful arrangement.

Accent Color
Green, plum, and purple with
chartreuse accent

Begonia, Blazing star, Hellebore,
Grapes, Snake's head fritillary

Find common patterns among
the elements. Here, the dots in
the begonia mirror the shape
of the grapes.

Analogous
Fuchsia, lilac, and plum

Fox's grape fritillary, Persian fritillary, Calla lily, Orchid, Dutch iris

Embrace negative space as form. Here, the space allows the flowers to appear as though they are dancing out of the vessel.

Accent Color
Silver green with plum
and mauve accents

Begonia, Lisianthus, Kangaroo
paw, Astrantia, Blackberry,
Ovens wattle, Honey myrtle

Face flowers, meaning your
showstoppers, are not limited
to florals. Here, decorative
leaves replace them.

Accent Color
Plum, chartreuse, and brown with amethyst accent

Cymbidium orchid, Lady's slipper orchid, Hellebore, Sweet pea, Thunberg spirea

Use florals from the same family. Here, multiple varieties of orchids—all strikingly different—come together to form a vibrant arrangement that still appears cohesive.

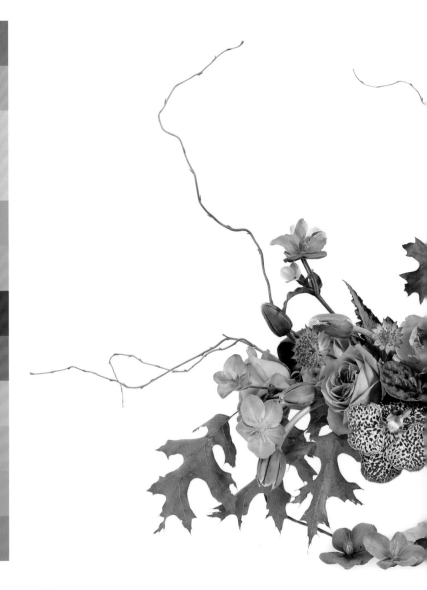

Analogous
Mauve, dusty rose, and sienna

Vanda orchid, Rose, Hellebore,
Oak, Corkscrew willow, Tulip

Focusing solely on color rather
than the specific elements
can lead to pleasant surprises.
Here, the knitting together
of oak leaves and orchids of
the same color family creates
a harmonious pairing.

Accent Color
Butter yellow and yellow
with scarlet accent

Coral bush, Tulip, Oncidium
orchid, Hellebore, Poppy,
Anthurium

For a contemporary look, add a
pop of color and play with shape
in unexpected ways. The intense
line of the textured scarlet
breaks up the yellow, creating
an asymmetrical balance.

Accent Color
Yellow with sienna accent

Ranunculus, Tulip, Daffodil,
Lemon, Sweet pea, Kumquat

A wide and shallow vessel with
a floral frog provides ample space
for textural elements like fruit,
adding layers to the arrangement.

Accent Color
Yellow and gray with
apricot accent

Daffodil, Mimosa, Rose,
Spanish moss, Mountain laurel
branch, Cecropia leaf

The haunting beauty of the
dripping moss brings another
element to a composition.
Added last, it acts as an ethereal
overlay of texture.

Complementary With Accent
Yellow and plum with
pale blue accent

Daffodil, Sweet pea, Pansy,
Mountain laurel branch

Display unexpected elements.
The daffodil bulb serves as
the focal point, with its roots
creating texture.

Accent Color
Yellow with pale blue accent

Mimosa, Daffodil,
Sweet pea, Lemon

Yellow is cheerful and warm.
Accented with the freshness
of pale blue, the floral
arrangement has the perfect
palette for summer.

Analogous
Yellow, orange, fuchsia, and red

Crown imperial fritillary,
Heliconia, Poppy, Tulip, Daffodil,
Oncidium orchid, Mimosa,
Ranunculus, Pansy, Hellebore

Hanging heliconia enhances
the arrangement, cascading
theatrically out of the vessel.

Triadic
Red, yellow, and blue

Tulip, Ranunculus, Muscari, Daffodil, Fox's grape fritillary, Globe allium

The combining of different colors creates a compositional balance in a painterly way. Make sure there are connecting hints of colors throughout.

Triadic
Red, yellow, and blue

Delphinium, Ranunculus,
Zinnia, Goldenrod,
Strawflower, Cornflower

Using primary colors is one of
the easiest ways to make a bold
statement. The absence of
subtlety directs the arrangement.

Complementary
Yellow and purple

Delphinium, Dahlia,
Oncidium orchid, Ranunculus,
Grapes, Plum, Rose

Black grapes and plums
add punctuation, bringing
texture to the composition.
Used in moderation, they
offer visual breaks.

Accent Color
Yellow with purple accent

Oncidium orchid, Rose,
Vanda orchid, Wax flower,
Cape gooseberry, Dried grass

To emphasize asymmetry, use
an accent color. Here, purple
orchids are offset to one side
of the composition.

Accent Color
Yellow, gold, and orange with
black accent

Oncidium orchid, Ranunculus,
Palm nut

Play with verticality in your design.
The contrast between upright
florals and the cascading elements
distinguishes this arrangement.

Accent Color
Brown with yellow accent

Lemon, Pampas grass, Muscari,
Poppy pod, Dried grass

Instead of face flowers,
substitute fruit, such as citrus,
grapes, and pomegranates,
for an unexpected design.

Analogous
Yellow, pale yellow,
and chartreuse

Oncidium orchid, Beehive ginger,
Dahlia, Ranunculus, Wax flower,
Lemon, Ground cherry,
Dried grass

Using sprays of oncidium orchids
and fruit to create texture is
an easy way to enhance any
analogous color scheme.

Transitional
From brown to green

Peony, Oncidium orchid,
Cymbidium orchid, Tangerine,
Spirea leaf

Use fresh produce, such as
tangerines, to create subtle color
variations in an arrangement.

Accent Color
Pale green and chartreuse
with orange accent

Poppy, Hellebore, Amaranth,
Lichen-covered branch, Grapes

When using identical vessels,
break up the composition to
avoid uniformity, filling each
container with diverse florals
and colors.

Rainbow
Full spectrum of color in pastel
and saturated hues

Crown imperial fritillary, Pansy,
Poppy, Tulip, Daffodil, Hellebore,
Snake allium

To de-emphasize a rigid formal
structure, use strong gestural
florals. A wild composition creates
movement and evokes romance.

Rainbow
Full spectrum of color
in saturated hues

Tulip, Crown imperial fritillary,
Persian fritillary, Ranunculus,
Grapes, Muscari, Orange

The inspiration of Old Dutch
paintings is rendered here
with loose gestures, fruit,
and unlimited colors and
types of florals.

Accent Color
Green and silver green
with red-orange accent

Tulip, Dusty miller, Goldenrod,
Thunberg spirea, Wheat

An upward movement, created
by concentrating colors in
a linear pattern, lends an
arrangement optimism.

Monochromatic
Orange

Marigold, Heuchera, Zinnia,
Rose, Grass

Deconstructing an arrangement
into different vessels to create
one composition adds depth to
a monochromatic palette.

Analogous
Yellow orange, orange, and brown with chartreuse accent

Sunflower, Marigold, Zinnia, Heuchera, Rose, Ruscus

When using an analogous color scheme, arrange colors to create an ombré effect for a soft and seamless look.

Accent Color
Ocher and peach with
yellow-orange accent

Cymbidium orchid, Heliconia,
Ranunculus, Lisianthus, Grass

The heliconias's graphic shape
offers a contrasting silhouette
against delicate elements like
the ranunculus and grass.

Monochromatic
Brown

Dried banana leaf, Rose, Chrysanthemum, Cymbidium orchid, Wax flower, African tulip tree fruit pod, Ranunculus, Pampas grass, Privet berry

Dried banana leaves, or other large foliage, can act as a textural canvas. Use them as the foundation on which to build an arrangement with a strong silhouette.

Accent Color
Yellow orange, orange, and
peach with burgundy accent

Rose, Ranunculus, Tulip, Daffodil,
Scabiosa, Chocolate cosmos,
Juniper, Palm nut, Kumquat

To create a horizontal
arrangement, use a vessel with
a wide opening.

Triadic
Peach, blue, and gold

Dahlia, Larkspur, Carnation,
Privet berry, Palm nut, Olive,
Grass

Designing in a footed bowl or
compote allows an arrangement
to cascade over the vessel's rim,
creating movement.

Complementary
Yellow orange and pale blue

Rose, Larkspur, Tulip, Sweet pea, Kumquat, Golden lantern lily

Citrus fruit, like kumquats, introduce a bright and fresh touch to an arrangement.

Analogous
Yellow orange, orange, gold, and peach

Ranunculus, Tulip, Rose, Palm nut, Daffodil, Golden lantern lily, Sweet pea

Using transitional colors, such as peach and gold, as seen here, results in a successful analogous color scheme that allows the eyes to seamlessly wander from one color to the next.

Accent Color
Peach, beige, and pink
with coral accent

Heliconia, Ranunculus, Sweet
pea, Gerbera daisy, Rose,
Poinsettia

To strengthen a color palette,
do not insert greenery. Without
added distractions, the focus
is on pure color.

Accent Color
Gold, peach, and brown
with fuchsia accent

Anthurium, Dahlia, Sweet pea,
Eucalyptus, Palm nut, Cymbidium
orchid, Wheat

Warm colors, like gold and peach,
reflect the vivid sunshine of the
summer months. Use this palette
to brighten up dreary days.

Transitional
From fuchsia to cream

Peony, Rose, Lisianthus, Lacecap hydrangea, Dried silver grass

To add movement, incorporate vines that loosely hug the vessel as a finishing touch.

Accent Color
Peach, brown, and fuchsia
with burgundy accent

Anthurium, Dahlia, Phalaenopsis
orchid, Coralberry, Ranunculus

Use a vessel with a small
opening to create a loose and
gestural arrangement.

Accent Color
Yellow orange and gold
with fuchsia accent

Rose, Tulip, Ranunculus, Sweet
pea, Daffodil, Kumquat

The cluster of fuchsia roses,
a classic floral, on one side
of the arrangement gives the
composition an edgy look.
Then, in an unexpected turn,
the yellow-orange kumquats
soften the robust pinkness.

Analogous
Red, peach, orange, and purple

Poppy, Tulip, Ranunculus, Japanese quince

Instead of green foliage, use flowering branches to add another color element to an arrangement.

Transitional
From coral to apricot

Rose, Japanese quince, Tulip,
Sweet pea, Eucalyptus, Grevillea
'Pink Pokers', Wiry wattle

Delicate flowers can easily get
lost in the mix. Use negative
space to frame them in busier
areas. Here, the quince rises
from the crescent-shaped center
of the arrangement.

Analogous
Coral, pink, peach, and orange

Peony, Crown imperial fritillary,
Rose, Ranunculus, Jasmine,
Chamomile, Larkspur,
Japanese quince

Soft jasmine vine paired with
fully opened peonies adds
whimsy and movement.

Accent Color
Orange and coral with
lavender accent

Anemone, Tulip, Amaranth,
Sweet pea, Daffodil,
Thunberg spirea, Carnation

Cascading amaranth evokes the
feeling of water flowing from the
vessel, creating fluid movement
within an arrangement.

Analogous
Lavender, coral, butter yellow, and peach

Rose, Anemone, Sweet pea, Hyacinth, Strawflower, Fringed lavender, Mediterranean heather

When foliage and gestural elements, like branches, are not used, you can focus on color and the arrangement of the stems to create emotion.

Analogous
Scarlet, coral, and pink

Anthurium, Pansy, Cathedral bells, Japanese quince, Hellebore, Sweet pea, Tulip

Pansies include a multitude of colors in each bloom, making them perfect for use as transition colors.

Analogous
Peach, orange, and rust

Dahlia, Ranunculus, Tulip, Sweet pea, Rose, Persimmon, Heliconia, Grapes, Amaranth

Tulips easily add movement to an arrangement. You can gently bend their malleable stems to a desired gesture.

Analogous
Red orange, orange, and brown

New Zealand flax leaf, Tulip,
Rose, Ranunculus, Sweet pea,
Strawflower

Use large leaves as you would
a ribbon to polish off an
arrangement.

Accent Color
Red orange with lavender accent

Tulip, Stock, Lavender

Look to the shape of the primary
floral for inspiration. The shape
of the tulip is mirrored by the
explosive direction of the design.

Accent Color
Pink and magenta with
coral accent

Rose, Strawflower, Sweet
pea, Thunberg spirea, Tulip,
Mediterranean heather,
Poppy pod

A saturation of magenta paired
with jewel tones can be dark
and moody. If you prefer, combine
it with brighter hues, such as
pink and coral, to add vibrancy
and energy.

255

Accent Color
Scarlet with white accent

Anthurium, Japanese quince,
Ranunculus, Daisy

White as an accent color, even
when used minimally, helps
break up monochromatic
arrangements. Bold punctuation
is not always necessary.

Monochromatic
Coral

Rose, Sweet pea,
Ranunculus, Bromeliad

Coral is the perfect alternative
to red. It is just as impactful
but is not victim to familiar
associations, like red is with
holidays and romance.

Accent Color
Orange and yellow orange
with magenta accent

Bromeliad, Tulip, Rose,
Ranunculus, Sweet pea

With its shape and color, the
bromeliad looks both like a
flower and leaf, adding vibrancy
to a design.

Accent Color
Beige, pink, and fuchsia
with yellow accent

Ranunculus, Variegated
conebush, Dried grass

For a more contemporary design,
build a structure with grass and
reeds surrounding your florals.

Analogous
Red, orange, and yellow

Heliconia, Oncidium orchid,
Joseph's coat leaf, Ranunculus

Look to natural elements, like
fire here, to inspire both the color
and shape of an arrangement.

Transitional
From peach to rust

Dahlia, Ranunculus, Grapes,
Zinnia, Amaranth, Celosia,
Wax flower, Pomegranate,
Palm nut

To create the most painterly
arrangements, go for a strong
cascade of elements flowing
out from a vessel.

Accent Color
White with red accent

Rose, Ranunculus, Pampas grass

Red is an incredibly stimulating color. When used as an accent, especially contrasting white or cool colors, it energizes your composition.

Complementary
Rust and chartreuse

Garden cosmos, Snake allium,
Palm nut, Grass

Look to the shape of the vase
itself for inspiration. The sinuous
lines of florals mimic the vessel's
curves, resulting in a coordinated
composition.

Analogous
Beige, pink, and scarlet

Tulip, Carnation, Sweet pea,
Bleeding heart, Rose

Break away from using roses
as the centerpiece of an
arrangement. Bleeding hearts
can inspire romance, creating
soft falling movements
throughout a design.

Accent Color
Pink, orange, and red with
hot pink accent

Peony, Crown imperial fritillary,
Tulip, Ranunculus, Bleeding
heart, Lady's slipper orchid, Rose

Crown imperial fritillary can
act as both a face flower and
gestural element, bringing
movement and a focal point
to the arrangement.

Accent Color
White with fuchsia accent

Rose, Daffodil, Dragon fruit, Sweet pea, Ranunculus, Phalaenopsis orchid

Look for produce with unexpected patterns. Here, the inside of the dragon fruit complements the color palette of the florals, uniting the composition.

Accent Color
Fuchsia and pink with
yellow accent

Peony, Torch ginger, Ranunculus,
Sweet pea, Pepperberry

Accenting a stimulating color, like
fuchsia, with another stimulating
color, like yellow, heightens the
overall energy and impact.

Triadic
Golden yellow, pale blue,
and fuchsia

Rose, Ranunculus, Tweedia,
Oncidium orchid, Sweet pea,
Carnation

Placing florals in glass cloches
adds texture and an extra layer
to a composition. It creates
a contained wildness.

Accent Color
Peach, pink, and fuchsia
with pale blue accent

Torch ginger, Phalaenopsis
orchid, Heliconia, Anthurium,
Tweedia, Pepperberry, Sweet pea

When designing with a warm
palette, you can incorporate a
dash of blue as an accent color.
Here, appearing as an upward
diagonal, it creates a thoughtful
break in the arrangement.

Complementary
Rust and pale blue

Rose, Dried palm husk, Tweedia, Thistle, Dried grass, Cymbidium orchid

As seen here with the use of palm husk and dried grass, highly graphic elements can easily generate an arrangement. Bold lines make a strong statement.

Analogous
Peach, pink, and red

Phalaenopsis orchid, Heliconia,
Sweet pea, Croton leaf,
Dried branch

When you lack gestural elements,
include perpendicular branches
or foliage to increase height.

Accent Color
Brown, sienna, and pink
with black accent

Peony, Scabiosa, Chocolate
cosmos, Rose hip, Burning bush,
Carnation, Privet berry

Negative space creates
movement and energy within
an arrangement. Give gestural
elements room to breathe by
avoiding overcrowding.

Accent Color
Pink and burgundy
with brown accent

Poinsettia, Philodendron, Japanese
quince, Carnation, Teasel,
Eucalyptus, Tomato, Passion fruit,
Anthurium

Flowers do not always need to be
at the center of an arrangement.
Here, tomatoes and other produce
act as a focal point from which to
radiate out.

Analogous
Hot pink, burgundy, and red

Rose, Blood orange, Peach blossom, Amaranth, Variegated Indian shot leaf, Magnolia buds, Strawflower, Calathea leaf

There is always color inspiration inside of fruit, like the vivid burgundy and red of the blood orange here.

Analogous
Plum, magenta, and pink

Peony, Rose, Bleeding heart,
Sweet pea, Persian fritillary

Add large, attention-grabbing
florals, like pink peonies, to
create a linear visual break and
a balanced asymmetry.

Accent Color
White and green with
burgundy accent

Phalaenopsis orchid, Dahlia,
Camellia leaf

The center of phalaenopsis
orchids is often a striking color
like burgundy or yellow.
Use this characteristic to pull
other florals of a similar shade
into the arrangement.

Monochromatic
Magenta

Magnolia, Plum blossom

When working with only two
flower types, asymmetry results
in a noteworthy design.

Accent Color
Magenta with pale blue accent

Bromeliad, Tweedia

Opposites attracting is the key
to contrasting soft and sharp,
as seen here with the tweedia's
soft blooms and the bromeliad's
sharp edges.

Analogous
Fuchsia, pink, and amethyst

Anthurium, Peony, Cymbidium orchid, Ranunculus, Pepperberry, Dried branch

Clusters of berries, such as pepperberries, add texture and can unite vessels into a cohesive composition.

Analogous
Pink, fuchsia, purple, and blue

Sweet pea, Dahlia,
Tulip, Lisianthus,
Delphinium, Coralberry

Having flower faces, such
as the tulips here, mirror
or "look" at one another
creates compositional depth
and movement.

Accent Color
Red and burgundy
with pale blue accent

Rose, Sweet pea, Garden
cosmos, Palm nut

The cool pale blue is a strikingly
polar yet appealing contrast
to the warm red and burgundy.

Monochromatic
Red

Rose, Amaranth, Pomegranate

Red can be interpreted very subjectively and can appear dark and moody in an arrangement. By exploring the shape of the arrangement, it becomes more sultry than doleful.

Analogous
Blush, pink, rust, and burgundy

Rose, Garden cosmos,
Ranunculus, Hellebore,
Palm nut, Velvet bush

By not grouping colors together,
you create movement within
a composition made of multiples
of the same vessel.

Complementary
Red and green

Rose, Pitcher plant, Lady's slipper orchid, Shelf mushroom, String of pearls, Cork oak bark, Gold dust dracaena leaf, New Zealand flax leaf, Fern

Use variations of green and red to dissociate the familiar color combination from the winter holidays.

Transitional
From burgundy to cream

Amaryllis, Ranunculus, Rose,
Amaranth, Sweet pea, Juniper,
Wax flower, Cotoneaster berry,
Pomegranate

Draping amaranth around the
entirety of an arrangement brings
all the elements together and
elicits an ethereal feel.

Transitional
From fuchsia to purple

Dahlia, Philodendron,
Sweet pea, Ranunculus, Tulip,
Eucalyptus, Coralberry

Pair fuchsia with rich jewel tones
for a lavish arrangement.

Monochromatic
Fuchsia

Dahlia, Lisianthus, Sweet pea,
Ranunculus, Coralberry

To achieve a vivid appearance,
vary stem lengths and create
layers with the florals.

Accent Color
Brown with magenta accent

Anemone, Pitcher plant,
Teasel, Beech, Andromeda bud

Bring the seasons indoors with
your floral selections. Brown and
jewel tones are widely available
during the autumn months and
mirror the changing of the leaves.

Analogous
Dusty rose, lavender,
purple, and mauve

Rose, Anemone, Fringed
lavender, Sweet pea, Thunberg
spirea, Hellebore

Anemone is an ideal face flower.
Its center is very defined, offering
a moment of focus.

Accent Color
Lavender and white
with black accent

Scabiosa, Sweet pea, Hellebore,
Snake's head fritillary

Embrace subtle gestures.
The overall shape here mimics
the soft gestural tendrils of the
sweet pea, which were the initial
inspiration for the arrangement.

Analogous
Lavender, pale blue,
and silver green

Anemone, Hyacinth, Palm

When designing an arrangement,
consider where it will be displayed.
In entryways or on console
tables, the addition of palm or
another leaf to flowers can create
excitement, whereas the same
inclusion would not be successful
on a dining table due to its height.

**Monochromatic
Blue**

Larkspur, Thistle, Olive

This arrangement's lack of face
flowers creates a soft look,
with greater emphasis on texture
and gesture.

Accent Color
White, cream, and lavender
with lilac accent

Magnolia, Sweet pea, Tulip,
Ranunculus, Daffodil, Lupine,
Lilac, Snake's head fritillary

Incorporate accents that bring
both color and texture to an
arrangement, as the lilac does
here, adding softness.

Accent Color
Pale blue and beige
with magenta accent

Magnolia, Larkspur, Hellebore,
Rose, Lilac, Thunberg spirea

Add larger florals to the top
of the arrangement for an
appearance reminiscent of
a Flemish still life.

Analogous
Plum, mauve, and cream

Magnolia, Persian fritillary, Hellebore, Lilac, Naples onion, Eucalyptus

Incorporate striking contrasts in color, texture, and shape. The juxtaposition between the magnolia and dark foliage creates dimensionality.

Accent Color
Lavender, blush, cream, and
pale blue with black accent

Ranunculus, Sweet pea,
Tulip, Rose, Lisianthus,
Larkspur, Scabiosa,
Blackberry, Privet berry

A black accent adds
a contemporary edge
to soft pastels.

Accent Color
Plum, peach, and mauve
with apricot accent

Magnolia, Rose, Ranunculus,
Persian fritillary, Fox's grape
fritillary, Orchid, Daffodil

Incorporate contrasting
shapes into an arrangement
for a dynamic presentation.
For instance, the sharp points
of orchid petals here juxtapose
and balance the roundness
of magnolia flowers.

Accent Color
Yellow orange and peach
with lavender accent

Tulip, Torch ginger, Ranunculus,
Lilac, Grapefruit, White jasmine,
Pussy willow, Dutch iris, Lemon,
Willow

The rich citrus palette of yellow
orange and peach is extended
by adding grapefruit and lemons.

Analogous
Apricot, peach, pink, lavender, and purple

Torch ginger, Tulip, Hellebore, Rose, Heather, Bromeliad, Sweet pea

The eye-popping shape of the torch ginger becomes the focal point here and the arrangement's face flower.

Analogous
Lavender, lilac, and mauve

Lilac, Lupine, Lisianthus, Tulip,
Sweet pea, Corkscrew hazel

The tightness of this design
is broken up by the gestural
branches weaving through the
florals and thereby creating
movement.

Accent Color
Purple, lavender, and yellow
orange with peach accent

Tulip, Lisianthus, Rose,
Ranunculus, Heliconia, Privet
berry, Larkspur, Fringed lavender

Accent colors used outside of an
arrangement, deliberately placed
among the vases, direct the eye
to view the entirety of the design.

347

Triadic
Orange, lavender, and green

Tulip, Banana, Heliconia, Papaya,
Sugarcane, Bromeliad, Lilac,
Sweet pea, Rose, Persimmon,
Ground cherry

Incorporating tropical elements,
like sugarcane and banana,
increases graphic contrast
and texture.

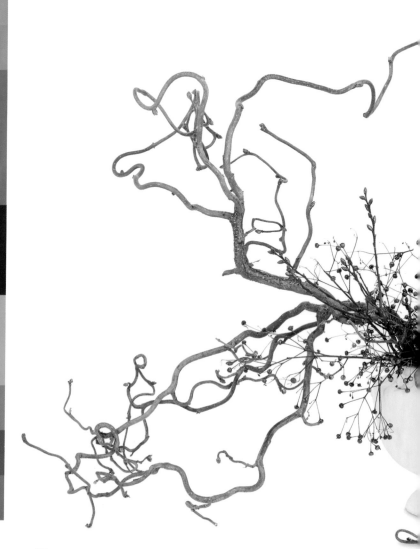

Analogous
Mauve, brown, and cream

Hellebore, Corkscrew hazel,
Toyon berry

Featuring corkscrew hazel
branches prominently and
unobstructed highlights the
power of this arrangement.

Analogous
Lilac, plum, purple, and mauve

Hellebore, Magnolia, Tulip, Lilac, Snake's head fritillary, Thunberg spirea, Begonia, Fig

Dark plums and blacks are unexpected colors to represent spring but are plentiful in the produce harvested at that time of year. Pair those colors with lilac and purple to soften the overall appearance.

Analogous
Lavender, lilac, purple, and plum

Rose, Ranunculus, Agonis, Vanda orchid, Plum, Pepino melon, Delphinium, Carnation, Aster, Phlox

When you hide the vessel under the flowers, the arrangement almost looks like a natural growth in the earth.

Analogous
Brown, burgundy, and purple

Calla lily, Sweet pea,
Philodendron, Olive fruit,
Eucalyptus

For a dramatic design, offset
the balance of an arrangement
with asymmetry—both vertically
and horizontally.

Accent Color
Brown, purple, and mauve
with lavender accent

Dried banana leaf, Rose,
Lisianthus, Tulip, Dried
silver grass, Flamboyant tree
seed pod, Privet berry

The brown in dried elements,
such as the leaves and seed
pods here, adds patina and
gravitas to an arrangement filled
with softer tones of lavender
and mauve.

Accent Color
Black with pink accent

Peony, Begonia, Calla lily,
Chocolate cosmos, Agonis, Privet
berry, Strawflower, Purple millet

To make a bold statement, create
a linear swath of an unexpected
color that runs through a
monochromatic arrangement.

Accent Color
Dark green and brown
with butter yellow accent

Ranunculus, Queen Anne's lace,
Cavolo nero kale, Philodendron,
Fern, Blackberry, Passion fruit

Using ferns throughout here
unifies the two arrangements
into one design.

Accent Color
Black and oxblood with
gray accent

Ranunculus, Calla lily, Lisianthus,
Privet berry, Mushroom, Scabiosa,
Blackberry

Gray is not a common color
in flowers, but it can be found
in mushrooms and bark. Use
these latter elements to add
a touch of lightness and texture
to a moody arrangement.

Monochromatic
Black with mauve accent

Calla lily, Begonia, Ranunculus, Agonis, Chocolate cosmos, Privet berry

In addition to flowers, use berries, grasses, and decorative leaves to tie an arrangement together.

Appendices

Color Theory Basics

For us, color is the key element in an arrangement. We always ask ourselves what color palette we want to work in before designing. Using basic color theory is a practical approach when starting out. By following any of these color schemes, you'll find that there are specific color combinations you can incorporate into your own designs.

Color Schemes

Accent Color
A color that is used for emphasis in an arrangement or composition

Analogous
A group of three to four colors next to each other on the color wheel

Complementary
Two colors that are directly opposite each other on the color wheel

Monochromatic
A single base hue

Rainbow
Soft-focus transitions between color, using all hues of the color wheel

Transitional
The gradual and seamless movement from one color to another

Triadic
A group of three colors evenly spaced on the color wheel. These include common combinations such as the primary (red, blue, and yellow) and secondary (orange, purple, and green) colors.

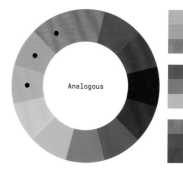

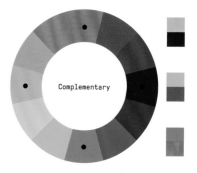

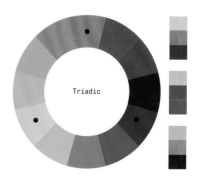

More Terms to Know

Cool palettes
Includes hues green through purple, including gray

Warm palettes
Includes hues red through yellow, including brown and beige

Hue
A color

Tint
The addition of white or lighter colors in a design

Shade
The addition of black or darker colors in a design

Tone
The addition of either black or white to a hue

Saturation
The intensity, or dominance, of a color

Undertones
The nondominant color in a flower; a hue that is subtle or faint

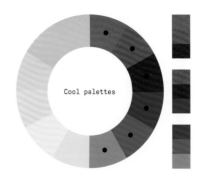

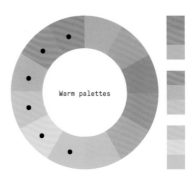

Glossary

Arrangement
A group of elements, such as flowers, foliage, and fruit, designed in one vessel

Asymmetrical
Having sides or aspects that are not equal in size or shape; lacking symmetry

Balance
An even distribution of visual weight of elements

Base structure
The elements in a composition or arrangement that create form; these are the first elements, usually foliage or branches, added to a design

Border
The outline or edge of a composition or arrangement

Cascade
A downward movement of an element over the edge of a vessel

Cohesive
When the elements in a design are unified and fit together well

Color blocking
Concentrations of like colors paired with contrasting colors, with no concern for matching

Composition
A display of elements made up of multiple vessels and ingredients

Contrast
Using opposite attributes, such as light and dark or textured and smooth, to create impact

Deconstruction
To pull apart elements that make a whole

Depth
Dimension, beyond shape, that gives a design form

Earthy
Soft hues commonly found in nature, especially its foundations and surfaces, including mud, grass, sand, bark, and stone

Emotion
A state of mind or feeling created within a design

Emphasis
An expression highlighting a specific area in a design

Energy
Strong contrast in color or movement

English garden style
A lack of contrived structure, leading to a wild and organic appearance; uses typical English garden flowers and elements

Ethereal
Light and delicate look with an otherworldly feel

Flemish
Having the look and feel of European still life paintings from the fifteenth to seventeenth centuries; includes the use of elements beyond flowers, foliage, and produce

Focal point
The center of interest in a design

Foliage
The leaves of a plant

Gestural
A sinuous and expressive movement of stems

Graphic
A vivid look with strong details

Impact
Having a strong emotional effect

Inspiration
A creative idea to do, create, or feel an emotion, often pulled from a source such as art or music

Juxtaposition
Placing two elements together to create a contrasting effect

Lightness
The use of pale colors and delicate elements

Lines
A long visual extent of an element or color

Minimalist
A design with few elements; best when discovered and not planned

Modern
Design that is current and relevant, often with strong visual impact and color

Mood
The emotion evoked by a design

Movement
A visual change of shape

Negative space
The space between and around elements in a design, not the elements themselves

Offset
Placing an element out of balance in the design

Old World
Having an antique look

Ombré
The gradual blending of one color to another

Flower Categories

Optimism
A joyous feeling often evoked by bright colors and upward movement

Painterly
Artistic; having qualities of a painting, such as color, form, and texture

Palette
The range of colors used in a design

Patina
Adding an aged look, often through the use of green or brown, to an arrangement or composition

Pattern
Any repeated elements used in a decorative design

Pop
A small burst of color

Punctuation
A flower or other element, such as fruit or branches, employed to create a visual break; use sparingly

Romantic
Lush and full design with strong movement and color

Rustic
Simple, unkempt design that is typical of the countryside; often made of foraged material

Seamless
Smooth and continuous, with no visual breaks between elements

Shape
The contour or outline of a design

Softness
Includes the use of fine texture and lack of graphic elements

Tablescape
An artistic arrangement of elements on a table used to create a composition

Texture
The tactile feel or appearance of an element or design

Theatrical
Expressive and impactful

Transparency
The ability to see through a design, often with the use of negative space

Tropical
Warm-climate flowers, foliage, and produce

Versatility
The ability to use an element within an arrangement in many different ways

Verticality
Upward movement in a design

Visual break
Moments in a design that allow the eye to pause and move through an arrangement or composition

Wild
Evokes the feeling of being in nature by using gesture and negative space

Face flowers
Provide the big statement in an arrangement; should be the largest blooms featured, such as dahlias, anemone, and peonies

Textural flowers
Add visual interest and complexity; includes flowers such as sweet peas, thistle, and lilac

Gestural stems
Add movement, depth, and shape within an arrangement; examples include tulips, crown imperial fritillary, and cymbidium orchids

Filler flowers
Create the base structure of the arrangement and are helpful for blending; includes roses, carnations, larkspur, and ranunculus

Useful Tips for Arrangements

Hydration is the essence of flower care. That's how they will stay fresh the longest.

Immediately bring the flowers home from the store and process them to prepare them for your arrangement.

To process, give all flower stems a fresh cut. They should be trimmed within an inch of the bottom of the stem or the desired length for your vessel. A 45-degree-angle cut allows for maximum water absorption.

Use sharp clippers; blunt blades will crush the stems and stop them from absorbing water. You want the cleanest cut that you can get.

Since residue bacteria will cause flowers to perish, keep buckets clean and disinfected with soap and water.

Use flower food in the water. You can use the packets that often come with flowers, but any brand will work. Flower food is essentially sugar, water, and antibacterial agent. It's used to feed the flowers and kill any bacteria in the water.

Before placing flowers in the water, remove all leaves that will sit below the waterline, otherwise the leaves will encourage bacteria growth that is harmful to the life of the flowers. Fewer leaves allow more water to go to the flower head for maximum hydration.

Cool water is best for all flowers, but if you want to accelerate hydration or the opening of flower buds before arranging, place them in warm water for up to one hour. Warm water is only effective for hard stems, such as roses and peonies. All soft-stemmed flowers must go immediately into cool water.

For woody-stemmed flowers, such as lilacs, and when using branches, prepare the lower two inches of the stems by shaving off the outer layer of bark, then cut upward into the stem several times for a shredded look.

All poppy stems need the bottom inch or two cauterized to seal in moisture. To do this, use a lighter or any other fire source before placing into the water.

In the spirit of good hydration, misting is very effective. This especially applies to hydrangeas. For poorly ventilated and overheated venues, misting will encourage your flowers to stay fresh longer.

Keep your arrangement in a cool place and away from a heavy draft. Heat will cause the flowers to wilt. An ideal room temperature is 68°F (20°C). If possible, avoid placing arrangements in direct sunlight.

For longer-lasting arrangements, change the water every three days. When doing this, add flower food, if available, to the new water. Be sure to keep the vessel full to prevent the flowers from drying out and wilting. Whenever a flower is removed from the water, a fresh angled cut needs to be made before returning it to the fresh water. When a stem is removed from the water, it will immediately begin to seal up, prohibiting further hydration when returned to the water.

Essential Tools

Wire floral netting
for use as mechanic for opaque vessels, such as footed bowls, compotes, trays, and urns

Floral wire
for both holding stems in specific shapes and attaching elements to one another

Floral clippers
for cutting flower stems and foliage; do not use them on any other materials as this will quickly make them blunt

Wire clippers
for cutting wire; it's very important that you do not use your floral clippers to cut wire

Green floral tape
for taping grids and holding mechanics in place; has a much stronger hold than clear floral tape

Clear floral tape
for use with more delicate applications and for glass vessels; do not substitute regular clear sticky tape, which is not as durable

Wood floral stakes
used for both putting produce in arrangements and lengthening the stems of flowers when paired with a water tube

Water tubes
used for stems that are not able to sit in water

Floral food
used to increase the longevity of flowers, this is a mixture of sugar, water, and antibacterial agent; it's essential and keeps the water clear and stimulates water uptake in flowers

Buckets
to hold flowers while they are waiting to be arranged; fill bucket one-third full with cold water and dilute with one tablespoon flower food

Floral pin frog (kenzan)
for use in more minimal designs, such as ikebana, or as added support to tape grids or wire netting

Floral putty
used to adhere a floral frog to a vessel

Vessel Recommendations

These are some of our favorite types of vessels to use when arranging. Select your vase based on the flowers you'll be working with and the look you're trying to achieve. To prepare the vases, we use a combination of wire floral netting, floral tape, and/or pin frogs.

Footed bowl
Allows for your arrangement to cascade heavily over the vessel's rim. In our opinion, this is the most versatile option. It also gives your arrangement an Old World feel. Because of the shallow nature of the bowl, a cage made of floral wire netting is the best option for mechanics. (1)

Compote
A smaller footed bowl that works well for delicate florals. Can be used for satellite arrangements paired with larger designs or as a centerpiece for minimalist tablescapes. (2)

Found vessels
Includes pitchers, cups, bowls, and more. These vessels can give your flowers a relaxed, effortless look. Cluster them together to make full compositions.

Bud vases
Can hold single stems or small clusters of flowers. These vessels are best for a simple approach to floral design. Can also be grouped together to make a larger composition.

Tall vase
Works well for branches and single-stem-variety arrangements. (3)

Shallow bowl
Use with floral pin frog. This vessel is used heavily in the art of ikebana. (4)

Urn
Use for large-scale arrangements to create impact.

(1)   (2)   (3)   (4)

Suggested Color Palettes

Seasonal

Spring
White, lavender, blush, peach, and pink

Summer
Yellow, orange, white, and blue

Autumn
Brown, peach, mauve, orange, and red

Winter
White, black, and plum

Events

Joyous Occasions
(such as a birthday
or celebration):
Yellow, pink, and blue

Serious Occasions
(such as a dinner party):
Plum, black, mauve, and white

Baby Showers
Pale blue, lavender, blush, and cream

Funerals
White, cream, and green

Weddings
(soft, dusty palette):
Mauve, lilac, brown, cream, and blush

(warm, citrus palette):
Peach, cream, pink, blush, and yellow

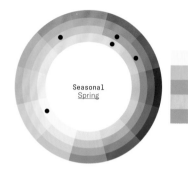

Seasonal
Spring

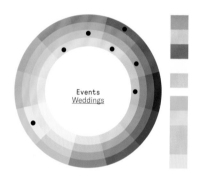

Events
Weddings

Wedding Flowers

A key part of our business is designing arrangements for weddings. Flowers are such an important aspect of the day, and we approach each wedding differently. When we meet with our clients, the first thing we find out is where they are getting married. You have to consider the venue. Is it indoors or outdoors, on a terrace or in a barn? At a hotel or in their home? Everything, including the floral arrangements, needs to be created around the space.

The next step is deciding on a color palette for the wedding. Consider your personal style and taste. Go into the space and see what colors are there. Is there wood? Is there gold on the ceiling? Metallic details in the light fixtures? When it comes to color, you don't want to fight a space. You want to work with it.

After you've selected the color palette, find ways to exaggerate the principles of the environment. The style of vases and the style of candles need to be cohesive. If you're getting married at the St. Regis, your decoration should be different from a beachside wedding.

You can't plan a wedding without thinking about the cost. Be realistic and consider how you want to allocate your budget. If you're obsessed with flowers, we recommend spending 20 percent of the overall design budget on florals. For a more standard affair, 5 to 10 percent would work perfectly. While taking costs into account is key, the most important thing is to have killer statements. You can get married on a terrace and have a showstopping event. No matter how much money you're spending, you have to create memorable moments.

To do this, you must first consider your guests. The least successful events are ones where the guests haven't been taken into account. What's your crowd like? What's the vibe? Keep this in mind to create experiences and environments that are compatible with your guests. Incorporate unforgettable moments with florals, such as site-specific floral installations. If a guest has an intimate experience in a lavish environment, they'll never forget it.

You can also create memorable moments with your tablescapes. We love tables filled with lots of flowers, glassware, and fruit, but you need to consider the event. What style table do you want? How is the food being served? Do you care about elements at eye level? Really think about the table you're creating. For round tables, place one graphic element in the center. We find that a low arrangement works best here. If you're using rectangular tables, we suggest including multiple elements that create one composition. On the following page, you'll find six different approaches to table decorating. Choose the approach that works best for your overall theme.

And, not to be forgotten, for bridal bouquets, think about the dress and your personal style. For a maximalist approach, go with a big and heavy cascade. For minimalist, choose a small bouquet. An important question to ask yourself: Do you want the bouquet to be the star of the show, or the dress? Go from there.

Tablescape Approaches

Minimalist

Use bud vases, candles, or ikebana-style arrangements. Keep it simple and have negative space on the table.

Maximalist

Feature an abundance of different elements, such as large arrangements paired with small satellite arrangements. The tables should be very flower-heavy, with individual florals being full and lush.

Painterly

Pair large arrangements with small arrangements. This approach is all about layers and adding fruit or produce on the tables. Look to Old World, Flemish, Romantic, and Baroque paintings for inspiration. Focus on heavy cascades of flowers and pulling the arrangements into the table itself, and play with different textures of vessels, such as glass paired with metal.

Rustic

Make the tablescape look like the countryside or a picnic in a garden or vineyard. Incorporate lots of wildflowers and texture. Use found vessels, pitchers, and cups.

Modern

Think of your table as an abstract painting. This approach is all about color blocking and working with line. Don't limit yourself to flowers. Play with color in tableware.

Garden Style

Think of the table as growing in your garden. The approach should be wild and romantic, with a lot of organic movement in the elements. Incorporate different floral elements, such as cut flowers, and beautiful gestural movements.

Color and Emotion

Every color evokes an emotion. Every color can transform the feeling of a space. It's incredibly subjective how a color can make you feel, but there are some general rules for what color can convey and how to use it in your floral arrangements.

It's all about the atmosphere. What are you trying to put out there? Is it a festive occasion? Is it a business dinner? Are you mourning the loss of someone? Are you celebrating the season? Are you formalizing something that was casual?

Flowers for a birthday party for someone who is high energy? Do something that's punctuated with color and not too soft. On the other hand, for a destination wedding in the tropics, by all means celebrate the colors of the place with crazy, vibrant, punctuated arrangements. If it's a romantic summer wedding in New England, try soft peach, pink, and white. A wedding in a vineyard, then use mostly wildflowers, as they are always a mix of colors.

The first rule is to consider what feeling you want to evoke with this occasion that you're doing the flowers for. Another rule is to find inspiration. It's not just about the feeling. Are you doing an event inspired by something? Are you hosting a Marie Antoinette–inspired party that's very Versailles, or are you doing a country dinner? Think of places, think of historical figures. Find inspiration in unexpected sources.

Being inspired by art is key for us. Kandinsky's artwork always moves us. Reference paintings and the colors used, and go from there. Music can be the inspiration too. When you listen to music, close your eyes. What colors do you see?

The biggest faux pas is creating something that is disjointed. Whatever you're designing needs to be cohesive. Don't fight against it. Try to keep the general family of design and color moving in the same direction.

Finally, we are done gendering color. If you're planning a baby shower, do something that celebrates the mother, not the baby. What are the mother's favorite flowers? What colors does she like?

For all events, think outside the box with themes. Execution is the most important element. And remember, different colors represent something unique to everyone, but there are some associations we find helpful when thinking about color and emotion. We keep these in mind when designing events for clients.

Color Associations

Red

The most powerful, yet most polarizing, color. There are a lot of associations tied to red, such as holidays and romance. Red can make a strong statement. It represents warmth, passion; it's angry, sensual. It's the color that pulls the most emotion out in a person. Works well as an accent color.

Pink

Evokes cheerful and happy feelings. It's soft, innocent, and calming.

Orange

Represents similar feelings as red, but not to the same extreme. Orange is warm, inviting. It's powerful and energetic. It falls easily into an autumnal, seasonal palette, but when paired with cool colors, it becomes perfect for the summer.

Yellow

Bright, happy, and joyous. When used in arrangements, yellow can elevate a mood. It's like sunlight. It's very fresh. We recommend using for any type of festive event.

Green

Very humble and down to earth. Green has properties that are cleansing of the mind and inner body. It represents a connection to nature. To us, a lack of greenery impoverishes the soul.

Blue

Blue is a very calming color. It's spiritual, subdued, soft, and peaceful. Blue does not make the same statement as warm colors. It presents a very cooling feeling. With its connection to the sky and water, blue is as cleansing as green. It is limitless.

Purple

An opulent and Old World color. It's seductive. Purple was commonly associated with royalty, as it used to be the hardest and most expensive pigment to procure. We also find purple to be a spiritual color.

White

The most innocent color, often used for weddings. White represents purity and cleanliness. For flowers, it is the least polarizing color. In some cultures, white can also represent mourning and religiosity.

Black

Dramatic and intense. Black adds punctuation and creates a boundary. It is sexy, moody, and seductive. It can be mysterious.

Brown

Represents something that is antique, Old World, and historical, like an old library. Brown can soften other colors and make a design feel lived in and storied.

Gold

Represents wealth and opulence. Gold is dazzling and very festive. It reminds us of Baroque art.

Silver

This color is glamorous, but it also represents permanence. There's a certain generational —or familial—aspect to silver.

Notes on Sustainability

The flower and events industry can be wasteful. When working with our clients, we prioritize following specific practices that can help sustainability. These costs should always be factored into your floral budget. If you can, shop local. Go to your local farmers' markets and flower farms when shopping for your arrangements. It's so important to support your community. We also recommend that you shop in season as much as possible.

When arranging flowers, try to have as minimal waste as possible. Reuse structures, and if you can, give flowers a second life through composting. For our events, we use Garbage Goddess, a New York–based green breakdown service that works toward zero-waste floral events. The company encourages sustainable practices in design prior to the event and will compost all organic floral material that was used and recycle or repurpose the other items. You can easily incorporate these steps into your own life. We highly recommend that you use a compost bin for your flowers at home. You can even make your own.

Repurposing flowers is another excellent way to be more sustainable—and make someone else's day. In larger cities, businesses like Repeat Roses take floral arrangements from events and transform them into bouquets to deliver to hospitals, nursing homes, and shelters.

Ultimately, it all comes down to waste. Be conscious of what you use and what you throw away. Avoid single-use materials. Small changes can make a big difference.

Color Swatches

In this section, we've included detachable color swatches to use when designing your own arrangements. The swatches correspond to the color bars that run along the side of each flower spread. On the back of the swatch, you'll find the caption information, as well as the page number where the arrangement can be found in the book. Tear out a few and take them with you when shopping at your local flower market. They're sure to provide plenty of color inspiration.

Black and White

Tulip, Ranunculus,
Anemone, Scabiosa,
Sweet pea,
Blackberry,
Privet berry

Shape and hard
lines, such as the
dramatic band
of black florals
running through the
arrangement, bring
interest and depth
to a black-and-
white design.

Accent Color
White and cream
with mauve accent

Ranunculus,
Snake's head
fritillary, Sweet pea

Using a subtle
checkerboard
pattern—as
this snake's
head fritillary
does—makes the
arrangement of
white florals pop.

Analogous
Silver, gray,
and white

Dusty miller,
Paper white,
Silver-painted fern,
Lichen-covered
branch

Use barren
branches to create
a hauntingly
beautiful silhouette,
perfect for the
winter months.

Accent Color
White with
green accent

Phalaenopsis
orchid, Sweet pea,
Olive, Wax flower

Olive branches
are a versatile
base available
year-round.
The soft green
pairs beautifully
with whites
and neutrals.

Accent Color
White and
cream with pale
green accent

Hellebore,
Ranunculus,
Daffodil, Tulip,
Thunberg spirea

The green of the
hellebore works
as an accent
color here. Always
consider the center
of florals as a part
of the color palette.

Monochromatic
White

Ranunculus, Dutch
iris, Bleeding heart,
Chamomile, Allium

Monochromatic
arrangements offer
creative freedom.
By focusing less on
color combinations,
you can place
emphasis on shape.

Complementary
Yellow and purple

Sweet pea, Tulip,
Pansy, Ranunculus,
Thunberg spirea

The geometry of
color blocking
brings a modern
touch to romantic
arrangements. Here,
the hint of yellow in
the white pansies
allows for a softer
color block.

Accent Color
Black and white
with silver-green
and lilac accents

Tulip, Calla lily,
Kalanchoe pumila

Calla lily and tulip
stems are incredibly
malleable and
relatively difficult
to break, allowing
you to manipulate
them for more
gestural expression.

Analogous
Gray, silver green,
and white

Begonia,
Ranunculus,
Rose, Sweet pea,
Paper white

Place large begonia
leaves—always a
great backdrop for
soft white flowers—
at the center of
a design.

Analogous
Silver green,
cream, and mauve

Hellebore,
Silver spear

Make an impact
with only two
elements by
manipulating
the foliage into
sculptural forms.

Analogous
Silver green,
gray, and white

Lichen-covered
branch, Calla lily

To create a
minimalist design,
let one element
inspire the shape,
like these lichen-
covered branches,
and build off it.

Accent Color
White with
pale blue and
yellow accents

Cecropia leaf,
Daffodil, Muscari,
Ranunculus, Pansy,
Pussy willow,
Thunberg spirea

Using a wide,
light-colored
element, such as
these leaves, as
the background
allows the flowers
to show off their
shape and color.

Analogous
White, purple,
mauve, and pink

Cecropia leaf,
Rose, Snake allium,
Ranunculus,
Thunberg spirea,
Kale

Wider designs
allow for the
presence of
negative space
at the center of
the arrangement.
Use this space to
spotlight delicate,
gestural stems.

Analogous
Gray, silver green,
and pale blue

Limonium, Dusty
miller, Tweedia,
Kalanchoe

Binding clusters
of elements,
such as Limonium,
with wire will
control the shape
and gesture of any
unruly actors in
your arrangements.

Accent Color
Silver green with
mauve accent

Rose, Ranunculus,
Limonium,
Kalanchoe pumila,
Thunberg spirea,
Muscari, Dusty
miller, Bergenia,
Poppy pod

When accenting
with a warm color,
use a silver-green
base as a softer
alternative to white.

Analogous
Mauve, cream,
and white

Hellebore,
Ranunculus, Snake
allium, Slender
velvet bush

Use gestural
elements, like
snake allium,
to form a border
around other
florals, creating a
design that is wild
yet contained.

Accent Color
Beige, plum,
and black with
apricot accent

Cymbidium orchid,
Cantaloupe,
Ranunculus,
Sweet pea, Rose,
Calla lily,
Privet berry

Color blocking
allows for
multiple points
of emphasis.
The inclusion
of large fruit,
such as the
cantaloupe here,
is an easy way to
create a brilliant
concentration
of color.

Analogous
Brown, peach,
and beige

Phalaenopsis
orchid, Wheat,
Variegated New
Zealand flax leaf

Minimalist
arrangements can
be just as impactful
as lush designs.
Focus emphasis
on a single line
or gesture.

Transitional
From gold to white

Phalaenopsis
orchid, Painted
cypress, Sweet pea

Break away from
traditional use of
red or green for
winter holiday
arrangements.
Metallic gold and
white can be just
as festive and are
more versatile.

Complementary
Beige and lavender

Carnation, Sweet
pea, Muscari,
Tweedia, Dried grass

Gather together
florals with
similar attributes.
Concentrations of
like flowers result
in an arrangement
with a more
natural look.

Monochromatic
Beige

Rose, Sweet pea,
Lisianthus, Wax
flower, Wheat

Having no
associations with a
specific holiday or
special event, beige
is a neutral color,
perfect for any time
of the year.

Transitional
Apricot, cream,
butter yellow,
and chartreuse

Rose, Tulip,
Ranunculus,
Corkscrew hazel,
Fig, Eucalyptus,
Daisy

Use figs for
punctuation in
lighter-hued
designs. When cut
open, they reveal
apricot, brown,
and pink tones
that meld well with
the color scheme.

Accent Color
Beige, yellow,
and brown with
sienna accent

Goldenrod,
Eucalyptus, Rose,
Phalaenopsis
orchid, Wax flower,
Western red cedar

Consider the color
of stems as part of
the overall palette.
The goldenrod
and eucalyptus
stems here add an
earthy tone to the
composition.

Monochromatic
Blush

Tulip, Rose,
Sweet pea,
Lisianthus, Nerine

Sweet pea, with
its soft color and
texture, adds a
delicate touch
that brings a
romantic look
to arrangements.

Accent Color
Pink and blush
with silver accent

Rose, Anthurium,
Dusty miller,
Japanese quince,
Silver-painted fern

A silver metallic
accent always gives
a composition a
ceremonious and
theatrical look.

Accent Color
Blush with
scarlet accent

Rose, Lisianthus,
Tulip, Rhubarb,
Sweet pea

Find a way to move
color throughout
an arrangement.
The red of the
rhubarb directs the
eye from the red
roses to the rest
of the composition.

Accent Color
Peach, cream, and
blush with dusty
rose accent

Rose, Tulip,
Hellebore, Olive,
Sweet pea,
Cathedral bells,
Thunberg spirea, Fig

Olive branches
are a wonderful
alternative to
pure green foliage
to soften a
palette. The silver
undertones work
beautifully with the
warm hues.

**Transitional
With Accent**
From pink to cream
with blue accent

Tulip, Ranunculus,
Rose, Thunberg
spirea, Sweet pea,
Stock, Muscari

Add an accent
color to the lighter-
toned side of an
arrangement.
It balances
out the overall
design, increasing
its impact.

Transitional
From blush
to pale blue

Rose, Sweet
pea, Larkspur,
Ranunculus,
Lisianthus,
Clematis, Nerine

The use of glass
vases offers
transparency,
making stems
important players
in the arrangement.
Use the deeper-
hued stems to
create a stark
contrast to the
pastel petals.

Accent Color
Pink with pale blue
and black accents

Rose, Sweet pea,
Muscari, Lavender,
Eucalyptus,
Philodendron
'Imperial Red',
Fringed lavender

Add a dark dash
of color to a bright
pastel palette to
inject intensity to
the arrangement.

Accent Color
Blush, peach,
and cream with
purple accent

Poppy, Rose,
Anemone, Tulip,
Sweet pea,
Flowering cherry

When working
with two vessels,
create continuity
in the shape of
the arrangements.
This helps pull them
together, making a
single vignette.

Accent Color
Blush and pink
with black accent

Philodendron
'Imperial Red', Tulip,
Ranunculus, Rose,
Plum blossom

Florals with a
wide face, like the
philodendron, can
act as the base
structure and
showcase the
other elements in
the arrangement.

Monochromatic
Pink

Peony, Rose,
Ranunculus,
Corkscrew
willow, Amaranth,
Strawflower,
Emerald ripple
peperomia,
Lisianthus

To create
a horizontal
composition with
vertical vessels,
keep florals
low and wide,
incorporating
cascading
elements, such
as amaranth and
corkscrew willow.

Analogous
Cream, pink,
and blush

Tulip, Bromeliad,
Rose, Ranunculus,
Sweet pea,
Carnation,
Calathea leaf

Pair spring flowers
with warm-climate
elements, such
as bromeliads, for
a tropical feeling.

Analogous
Pink, peach,
and apricot

Peony, Ranunculus,
Sweet pea, Rose,
Bleeding heart,
Chamomile,
Daffodil, Thunberg
spirea

Bright pastels,
like peach and
apricot, are cheerful
and uplifting. As
analogous colors,
this combination
ensures a seamless
appearance.

Transitional
From butter yellow
to pink

Poinsettia, Rose,
Anthurium,
Japanese quince,
Tulip, Hellebore,
Ranunculus, Daisy

A poinsettia can
be used as both
a base foliage and
a focal element.
The colorful leaves,
with hints of pink
and yellow, unite
the composition.

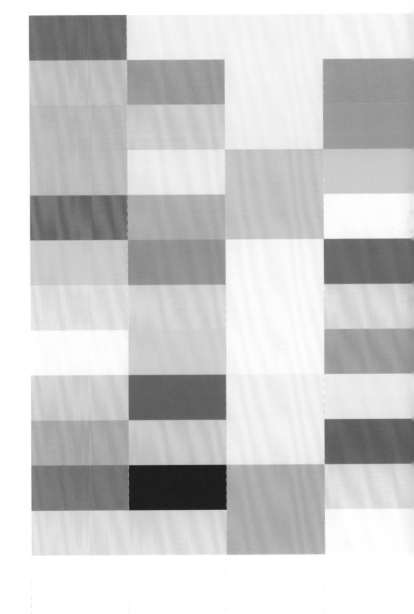

Analogous
Pink, blush, cream,
peach, and yellow

Poppy, Tulip,
Hellebore, Snake's
head fritillary,
Daffodil, Sweet pea

Using florals
of a similar tone
heightens the
seamlessness
of an analogous
design and is
gentler on the eye.

Complementary
Peach and
pale blue

Carnation

When creating a
composition with
only one type of
flower, focus on
color variation
and the desired
shape of the
arrangement.

Accent Color
Orange, brown,
and peach with
burgundy accent

Crown imperial
fritillary, Tulip,
Blood orange,
Ranunculus,
Eucalyptus,
Pussy willow

Employing vessels
made of different
materials, like glass
and ceramic here,
adds texture
to a composition.

Complementary
Peach and
pale blue

Tulip, Ranunculus,
Daffodil, Muscari,
Sweet pea, Statice,
Rose

Add blue to
arrangements
with warm colors.
Inspired by old
Flemish paintings,
this design features
a touch of contrast
with the blue
Muscari, making the
other florals pop.

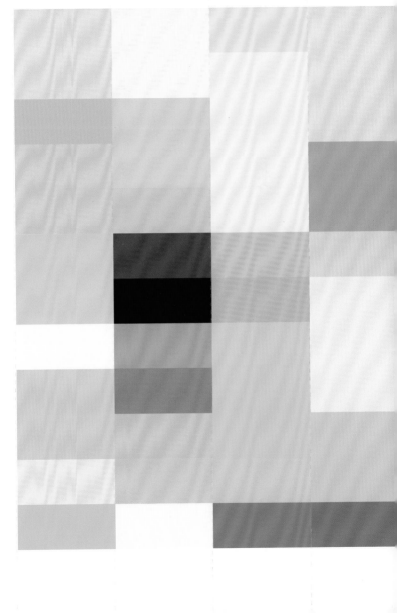

Transitional
From chartreuse
to beige

Rose, Lady's
slipper orchid,
Ivy, Lisianthus,
Sweet pea, Western
red cedar, Wheat

A loose, textural,
rambling element,
like ivy, always
evokes a certain
English-garden
feeling.

Complementary
Peach and
chartreuse

Ginger, Coconut,
Anthurium, Grass,
Poppy, Goldenrod,
Palm nut

This arrangement
works because
of its strong use
of texture. Each
element is unique
in character, but
the components
come together
beautifully to create
a cohesive design.

**Analogous
With Accent**
Peach, yellow
green, and pale
blue with purple
accent

Poppy, Anemone,
Muscari, Anthurium,
Sweet pea

Adding a dark
punctuation to a
simple arrangement
immediately makes
it more interesting
and dynamic. Here,
a purple accent
within the light
analogous palette
creates energy.

Accent Color
Yellow and pale
green with
pink accent

Plum blossom,
Forsythia, Grapes,
Tulip, Daffodil,
Rose, Lemon

Incorporate
several varieties
of flowering
branches, such
as plum blossom
and forsythia, in a
single composition
to add strong lines
of energy to
the arrangement.

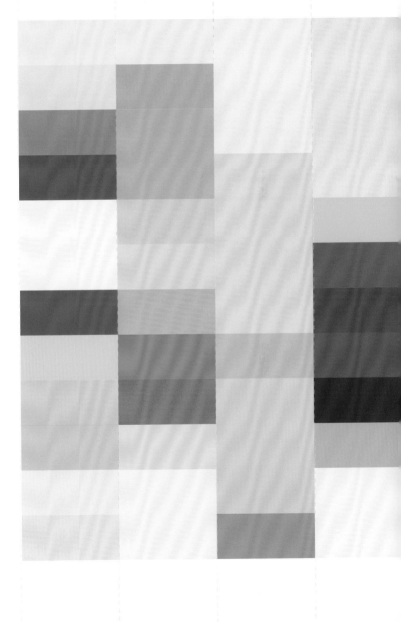

Monochromatic
Dusty purple

Dutch iris, Lilac, Rose, Lupine

In a monochromatic design, staggering the heights of the elements helps create vertical movement and depth.

Accent Color
Lavender with cream accent

Asparagus, Sweet pea, Clematis

Give people something to talk about by inserting unusual produce, like cream-colored asparagus, into your design.

Accent Color
Lavender with coral accent

Stock, Sweet pea, Rose, Tulip, Limonium, Kalanchoe pumila

Long linear swaths of color always break up a monochromatic palette, sending the eye in pleasing directions.

Accent Color
Pale blue and blue with blush accent

Rose, Muscari, Larkspur, Globe allium, Sweet pea

Find inspiration in unexpected places—or people. Inspired by Marie Antoinette, this arrangement incorporates her penchant for pale blue and blush and evokes a French court.

Analogous
Pale blue, blue,
and purple

Muscari, Larkspur,
Love-in-a-mist,
Anemone

Color-block
florals in simple
arrangements to
make them appear
more dynamic.

Analogous
White, yellow,
and green

Daffodil,
Ranunculus,
Variegated Japanese
silver grass

For a purposefully
untamed look,
manipulate the
grass to encircle
the florals,
encaging them
within its blades.

Monochromatic
Pale green

Lisianthus,
Lady's slipper
orchid, Carnation,
Cymbidium orchid,
Cypress branch

For an arrangement
with a bright
and youthful
energy, introduce
pale green.

Accent Color
Chartreuse,
pale green, and
orange with yellow-
orange accent

Lady's slipper
orchid, Lisianthus,
Daffodil, Orange,
Cymbidium orchid,
Eucalyptus pod, Ivy

Household vessels,
such as pitchers
and mugs, offer
an effortless and
rustic look.

Accent Color
Pale green and
chartreuse
with purple accent

Vanda orchid,
Sweet pea, Poppy,
Grapes, Palm nut,
Pepperberry

Be creative
with how you
incorporate green
elements. Rather
than using only
foliage, try grapes
or palm nuts for
an added punch.

Accent Color
Green, pale green,
and chartreuse
with pale
blue accent

Calathea leaf,
Larkspur,
Globe allium,
Chrysanthemum,
Coconut,
Goldenrod, Globe
artichoke, Grapes,
Muscari

Use the patterns
within nature
as a tool. The
marbled, sharp
lines of the foliage
juxtaposed with
the soft colors of
the florals create
vibrancy.

Complementary
Pale green
and blush

Poppy, Sweet pea,
Hellebore, Fern,
Palm nut, Bergenia

Incorporating
elements that
offer movement
will make a simple
arrangement
more impactful.

Monochromatic
Butter yellow

Peony, Rose,
Tulip, Ranunculus,
Passion vine,
Dumb cane leaf,
Queen Anne's lace,
Daffodil bulb

Here, a vine
weaves in a circular
path around the
entirety of the
composition and
between the
dissimilar vessels,
making them feel
like one.

Accent Color
Butter yellow with
dark green accent

Rose, Hellebore,
Tulip, Cavolo
nero kale,
Ranunculus, Fern

A backdrop of dark
foliage contrasts
with lighter-hued
florals, showcasing
the flowers
and emphasizing
their beauty.

Accent Color
Green with
white accent

Peppergrass, Iris,
Bleeding heart

Make movement
the focus of an
arrangement.
Here, the sinuous
gestural lines
of the expressive
peppergrass
add allure.

Analogous
White, cream,
and brown

Ranunculus,
Daffodil, Hellebore,
Dwarf crown
imperial fritillary,
Eucalyptus

Break up green
florals with touches
of brown. Acting
as a patina, it gives
the arrangement
the look of an Old
World painting.

Analogous
Peach, cream,
and apricot

Palm, Anthurium,
Rose, Daffodil

A floral frog has
only so much real
estate. Focus on
adding strong
individual elements
rather than
clustering a
handful of florals.

Monochromatic
Green

Begonia,
Pallid fritillary,
Huckleberry,
Fern, Rosemary

To add depth to
any monochromatic
arrangement, mix
up the color's
tones, as seen
here with the
range of greens.

Accent Color
White with silver-
green accent

Palm, Daffodil,
Ranunculus,
Thunberg spirea,
Sweet pea, Tulip

To help white
florals pop, arrange
them in front of
large, graphic
leaves, such as
palm fronds.

Accent Color
Pale green and
green with
plum accent

Hellebore, Dwarf
crown imperial
fritillary, Fig,
Tulip, Privet berry,
Paper white

Break up bright
colors in an
arrangement
by using black
and plum as
punctuation points.

Accent Color
White and black
with brown accent

Protea, Calla lily,
Pampas grass,
Ranunculus,
Muscari, Snake's
head fritillary

When you
substitute grass
in place of
branches, it adds
an additional layer
of texture and sets
the shape of an
entire arrangement,
as seen here.

Monochromatic
Green

Alocasia, Pitcher
plant, Lady's
slipper orchid,
Fern, Grass, String
of pearls

A composition
made almost
exclusively of
foliage is just
as impactful
as one of flowers.
Employ leaves
with interesting
colors and patterns
for variety.

Analogous
Green, pale green,
chartreuse, and
butter yellow

Poppy, Begonia,
Daffodil, Fragrant
sumac

Here, the shape of
the poppies mimics
the spots on the
begonia, gathering
the elements
together.

Accent Color
Silver with
orange accent

Heliconia,
Eucalyptus,
Dusty miller,
Persimmon,
Papaya, Juniper,
Grapes, Rose

It's acceptable
to create
arrangements with
or without just
one type of flower.
Here, the focus is
on the foliage, with
the heliconia floral
serving as a pop
of color.

Accent Color
Chartreuse and
ocher with butter
yellow accent

Anthurium, Rose,
Sweet pea, Tulip,
Thunberg spirea

Incorporate
elements with like
colors. The ocher
in the anthurium
mirrors the ocher
of the sweet pea,
unifying the
color palette.

Monochromatic
Chartreuse

Anthurium, Lady's
slipper orchid,
Cymbidium orchid,
Vanda orchid,
Porcini mushroom,
Asparagus,
Palm nut

Mushrooms or
other fungi can
be an unexpected
element in
a composition.
They come in
a variety of colors,
such as white, red,
and yellow, and
can work in nearly
any design.

Accent Color
Chartreuse and
pale green with
plum accent

Anthurium,
Amaryllis, Lady's
slipper orchid,
Cymbidium orchid,
Calla lily, Scabiosa,
Ranunculus,
Grapes, Palm nut,
Blackberry

When possible,
source handmade
glass vessels.
The material has
more warmth
than their
mass-produced
counterparts, and
its imperfections
can add a unique
element to a
composition.

Complementary
Plum and yellow

Poppy, Forsythia,
Persian fritillary,
Dutch iris, Daffodil

To evoke the
relaxed feel of
a spring garden,
group iris and
forsythia together.

Accent Color
Plum, sienna, and
silver green with
yellow accent

Strawflower,
Begonia,
Lisianthus, Persian
fritillary, Sweet
pea, Kangaroo
paw, Goldenrod,
Eucalyptus

Accent colors do
not need to be
concentrated in
a single area. Here,
the yellow florals
are sprinkled
throughout to
allow your attention
to travel within
the design.

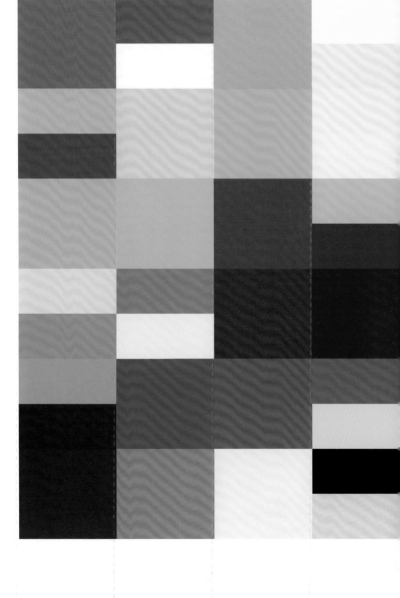

Accent Color
Burgundy and
blush with
chartreuse accent

Anthurium,
Ranunculus,
Rose, Sweet pea,
Tulip, Cherry
blossom, Palm nut,
Pepperberry

Position
concentrations of
color in overlapping
lines, creating
a focal point
where the two
colors cross. The
result is a bold
and impactful
arrangement.

Accent Color
Green, plum,
and purple with
chartreuse accent

Begonia, Blazing
star, Hellebore,
Grapes, Snake's
head fritillary

Find common
patterns among the
elements. Here, the
dots in the begonia
mirror the shape
of the grapes.

Analogous
Fuchsia, lilac,
and plum

Fox's grape
fritillary, Persian
fritillary, Calla lily,
Orchid, Dutch iris

Embrace negative
space as form.
Here, the space
allows the flowers
to appear as
though they are
dancing out of
the vessel.

Accent Color
Silver green
with plum and
mauve accents

Begonia,
Lisianthus,
Kangaroo paw,
Astrantia,
Blackberry,
Ovens wattle,
Honey myrtle

Face flowers,
meaning your
showstoppers,
are not limited
to florals. Here,
decorative leaves
replace them.

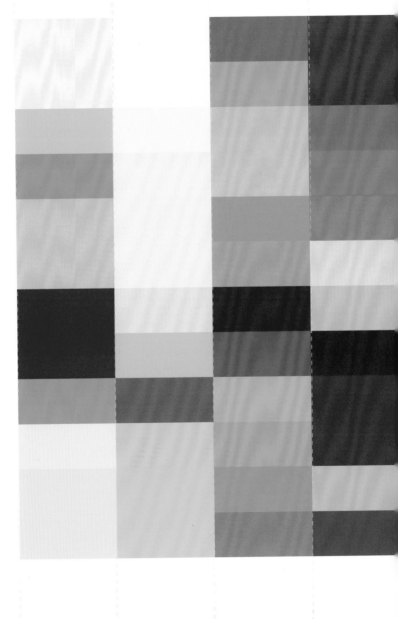

Accent Color
Plum, chartreuse,
and brown with
amethyst accent

Cymbidium orchid,
Lady's slipper
orchid, Hellebore,
Sweet pea,
Thunberg spirea

Use florals from
the same family.
Here, multiple
varieties of
orchids—all
strikingly different—
come together
to form a vibrant
arrangement
that still appears
cohesive.

Analogous
Mauve, dusty rose,
and sienna

Vanda orchid, Rose,
Hellebore, Oak,
Corkscrew willow,
Tulip

Focusing solely
on color rather
than the specific
elements can
lead to pleasant
surprises. Here, the
knitting together
of oak leaves and
orchids of the same
color family creates
a harmonious
pairing.

Accent Color
Butter yellow
and yellow with
scarlet accent

Coral bush, Tulip,
Oncidium orchid,
Hellebore, Poppy,
Anthurium

For a contemporary
look, add a pop
of color and play
with shape in
unexpected ways.
The intense line of
the textured scarlet
breaks up the
yellow, creating
an asymmetrical
balance.

Accent Color
Yellow with
sienna accent

Ranunculus,
Tulip, Daffodil,
Lemon, Sweet pea,
Kumquat

A wide and shallow
vessel with a floral
frog provides ample
space for textural
elements like fruit,
adding layers to
the arrangement.

Accent Color
Yellow and gray
with apricot accent

Daffodil, Mimosa,
Rose, Spanish
moss, Mountain
laurel branch,
Cecropia leaf

The haunting
beauty of the
dripping moss
brings another
element to a
composition.
Added last, it acts
as an ethereal
overlay of texture.

**Complementary
With Accent**
Yellow and plum
with pale blue
accent

Daffodil, Sweet pea,
Pansy, Mountain
laurel branch

Display unexpected
elements. The
daffodil bulb
serves as the focal
point, with its roots
creating texture.

Accent Color
Yellow with pale
blue accent

Mimosa, Daffodil,
Sweet pea, Lemon

Yellow is cheerful
and warm.
Accented with
the freshness of
pale blue, the floral
arrangement has
the perfect palette
for summer.

Analogous
Yellow, orange,
fuchsia, and red

Crown imperial
fritillary, Heliconia,
Poppy, Tulip,
Daffodil, Oncidium
orchid, Mimosa,
Ranunculus, Pansy,
Hellebore

Hanging heliconia
enhances the
arrangement,
cascading
theatrically out
of the vessel.

Triadic
Red, yellow,
and blue

Tulip, Ranunculus,
Muscari, Daffodil,
Fox's grape fritillary,
Globe allium

The combining
of different
colors creates
a compositional
balance in a
painterly way.
Make sure there
are connecting
hints of colors
throughout.

Triadic
Red, yellow, and
blue

Delphinium,
Ranunculus,
Zinnia, Goldenrod,
Strawflower,
Cornflower

Using primary
colors is one
of the easiest
ways to make a
bold statement.
The absence of
subtlety directs the
arrangement.

Complementary
Yellow and purple

Delphinium, Dahlia,
Oncidium orchid,
Ranunculus,
Grapes, Plum, Rose

Black grapes
and plums add
punctuation,
bringing texture
to the composition.
Used in moderation,
they offer visual
breaks.

Accent Color
Yellow with purple
accent

Oncidium orchid,
Rose, Vanda
orchid, Wax flower,
Cape gooseberry,
Dried grass

To emphasize
asymmetry, use an
accent color. Here,
purple orchids are
offset to one side
of the composition.

Accent Color
Yellow, gold, and
orange with black
accent

Oncidium orchid,
Ranunculus,
Palm nut

Play with verticality
in your design.
The contrast
between upright
florals and the
cascading elements
distinguishes
this arrangement.

Accent Color
Brown with
yellow accent

Lemon, Pampas
grass, Muscari,
Poppy pod, Dried
grass

Instead of face
flowers, substitute
fruit, such as
citrus, grapes, and
pomegranates,
for an unexpected
design.

Analogous
Yellow, pale yellow,
and chartreuse

Oncidium
orchid, Beehive
ginger, Dahlia,
Ranunculus,
Wax flower, Lemon,
Ground cherry,
Dried grass

Using sprays of
oncidium orchids
and fruit to create
texture is an easy
way to enhance
any analogous
color scheme.

Transitional
From brown
to green

Peony, Oncidium
orchid, Cymbidium
orchid, Tangerine,
Spirea leaf

Use fresh produce,
such as tangerines,
to create subtle
color variations in
an arrangement.

Accent Color
Pale green and
chartreuse with
orange accent

Poppy, Hellebore,
Amaranth, Lichen-
covered branch,
Grapes

When using
identical vessels,
break up the
composition to
avoid uniformity,
filling each
container with
diverse florals
and colors.

Rainbow
Full spectrum of
color in pastel and
saturated hues

Crown imperial
fritillary, Pansy,
Poppy, Tulip,
Daffodil, Hellebore,
Snake allium

To de-emphasize
a rigid formal
structure, use
strong gestural
florals. A wild
composition
creates movement
and evokes
romance.

Rainbow
Full spectrum
of color in
saturated hues

Tulip, Crown
imperial fritillary,
Persian fritillary,
Ranunculus,
Grapes, Muscari,
Orange

The inspiration
of Old Dutch
paintings is
rendered here
with loose gestures,
fruit, and unlimited
colors and
types of florals.

Accent Color
Green and silver
green with red-
orange accent

Tulip, Dusty
miller, Goldenrod,
Thunberg spirea,
Wheat

An upward
movement, created
by concentrating
colors in a linear
pattern, lends
an arrangement
optimism.

Monochromatic
Orange

Marigold, Heuchera, Zinnia, Rose, Grass

Deconstructing an arrangement into different vessels to create one composition adds depth to a monochromatic palette.

Analogous
Yellow orange, orange, and brown with chartreuse accent

Sunflower, Marigold, Zinnia, Heuchera, Rose, Ruscus

When using an analogous color scheme, arrange colors to create an ombré effect for a soft and seamless look.

Accent Color
Ocher and peach with yellow-orange accent

Cymbidium orchid, Heliconia, Ranunculus, Lisianthus, Grass

The heliconias's graphic shape offers a contrasting silhouette against delicate elements like the ranunculus and grass.

Monochromatic
Brown

Dried banana leaf, Rose, Chrysanthemum, Cymbidium orchid, Wax flower, African tulip tree fruit pod, Ranunculus, Pampas grass, Privet berry

Dried banana leaves, or other large foliage, can act as a textural canvas. Use them as the foundation on which to build an arrangement with a strong silhouette.

Accent Color
Yellow orange,
orange, and
peach with
burgundy accent

Rose, Ranunculus,
Tulip, Daffodil,
Scabiosa,
Chocolate cosmos,
Juniper, Palm nut,
Kumquat

To create a
horizontal
arrangement,
use a vessel with
a wide opening.

Triadic
Peach, blue, and
gold

Dahlia, Larkspur,
Carnation, Privet
berry, Palm nut,
Olive, Grass

Designing in a
footed bowl or
compote allows
an arrangement
to cascade over
the vessel's rim,
creating movement.

Complementary
Yellow orange and
pale blue

Rose, Larkspur,
Tulip, Sweet pea,
Kumquat, Golden
lantern lily

Citrus fruit,
like kumquats,
introduce a bright
and fresh touch to
an arrangement.

Analogous
Yellow orange,
orange, gold,
and peach

Ranunculus, Tulip,
Rose, Palm nut,
Daffodil, Golden
lantern lily,
Sweet pea

Using transitional
colors, such as
peach and gold, as
seen here, results
in a successful
analogous color
scheme that
allows the eyes to
seamlessly wander
from one color to
the next.

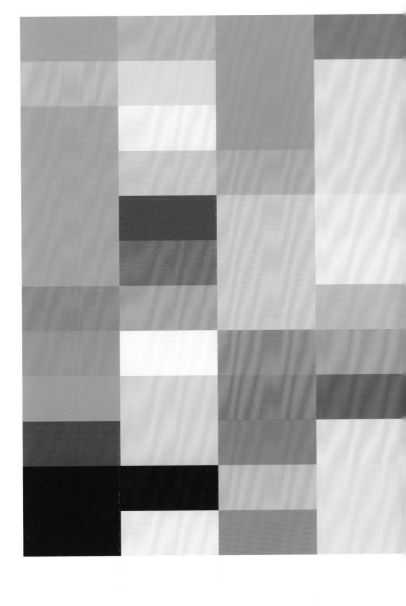

Accent Color
Peach, beige,
and pink with coral
accent

Heliconia,
Ranunculus,
Sweet pea,
Gerbera daisy,
Rose, Poinsettia

To strengthen
a color palette,
do not insert
greenery. Without
added distractions,
the focus is on
pure color.

Accent Color
Gold, peach,
and brown with
fuchsia accent

Anthurium,
Dahlia, Sweet
pea, Eucalyptus,
Palm nut,
Cymbidium orchid,
Wheat

Warm colors, like
gold and peach,
reflect the vivid
sunshine of the
summer months.
Use this palette
to brighten up
dreary days.

Transitional
From fuchsia
to cream

Peony, Rose,
Lisianthus, Lacecap
hydrangea, Dried
silver grass

To add movement,
incorporate vines
that loosely hug
the vessel as a
finishing touch.

Accent Color
Peach, brown,
and fuchsia with
burgundy accent

Anthurium, Dahlia,
Phalaenopsis
orchid, Coralberry,
Ranunculus

Use a vessel with
a small opening
to create a loose
and gestural
arrangement.

Accent Color
Yellow orange
and gold with
fuchsia accent

Rose, Tulip,
Ranunculus, Sweet
pea, Daffodil,
Kumquat

The cluster of
fuchsia roses,
a classic floral,
on one side of the
arrangement gives
the composition
an edgy look.
Then, in an
unexpected turn,
the yellow-orange
kumquats soften
the robust pinkness.

Analogous
Red, peach, orange,
and purple

Poppy, Tulip,
Ranunculus,
Japanese quince

Instead of green
foliage, use
flowering branches
to add another
color element to
an arrangement.

Transitional
From coral
to apricot

Rose, Japanese
quince, Tulip,
Sweet pea,
Eucalyptus,
Grevillea 'Pink
Pokers', Wiry wattle

Delicate flowers
can easily get lost
in the mix. Use
negative space
to frame them in
busier areas. Here,
the quince rises
from the crescent-
shaped center of
the arrangement.

Analogous
Coral, pink, peach,
and orange

Peony, Crown
imperial fritillary,
Rose, Ranunculus,
Jasmine,
Chamomile,
Larkspur,
Japanese quince

Soft jasmine vine
paired with fully
opened peonies
adds whimsy
and movement.

Accent Color
Orange and coral with lavender accent

Anemone, Tulip, Amaranth, Sweet pea, Daffodil, Thunberg spirea, Carnation

Cascading amaranth evokes the feeling of water flowing from the vessel, creating fluid movement within an arrangement.

Analogous
Lavender, coral, butter yellow, and peach

Rose, Anemone, Sweet pea, Hyacinth, Strawflower, Fringed lavender, Mediterranean heather

When foliage and gestural elements, like branches, are not used, you can focus on color and the arrangement of the stems to create emotion.

Analogous
Scarlet, coral, and pink

Anthurium, Pansy, Cathedral bells, Japanese quince, Hellebore, Sweet pea, Tulip

Pansies include a multitude of colors in each bloom, making them perfect for use as transition colors.

Analogous
Peach, orange, and rust

Dahlia, Ranunculus, Tulip, Sweet pea, Rose, Persimmon, Heliconia, Grapes, Amaranth

Tulips easily add movement to an arrangement. You can gently bend their malleable stems to a desired gesture.

Analogous
Red orange, orange,
and brown

New Zealand flax
leaf, Tulip, Rose,
Ranunculus,
Sweet pea,
Strawflower

Use large leaves as
you would a ribbon
to polish off
an arrangement.

Accent Color
Red orange with
lavender accent

Tulip, Stock,
Lavender

Look to the shape
of the primary floral
for inspiration.
The shape of the
tulip is mirrored
by the explosive
direction of
the design.

Accent Color
Pink and magenta
with coral accent

Rose, Strawflower,
Sweet pea,
Thunberg spirea,
Tulip, Mediterranean
heather, Poppy pod

A saturation of
magenta paired
with jewel tones
can be dark and
moody. If you
prefer, combine
it with brighter
hues, such as
pink and coral,
to add vibrancy
and energy.

Accent Color
Scarlet with
white accent

Anthurium,
Japanese quince,
Ranunculus, Daisy

White as an accent
color, even when
used minimally,
helps break up
monochromatic
arrangements. Bold
punctuation is not
always necessary.

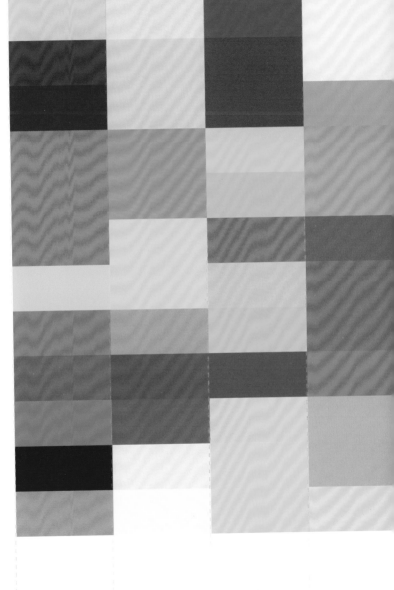

Monochromatic
Coral

Rose, Sweet pea,
Ranunculus,
Bromeliad

Coral is the perfect
alternative to
red. It is just as
impactful but is not
victim to familiar
associations, like
red is with holidays
and romance.

Accent Color
Orange and yellow
orange with
magenta accent

Bromeliad, Tulip,
Rose, Ranunculus,
Sweet pea

With its shape and
color, the bromeliad
looks both like a
flower and leaf,
adding vibrancy
to a design.

Accent Color
Beige, pink, and
fuchsia with
yellow accent

Ranunculus,
Variegated
conebush,
Dried grass

For a more
contemporary
design, build a
structure with
grass and reeds
surrounding
your florals.

Analogous
Red, orange,
and yellow

Heliconia,
Oncidium orchid,
Joseph's coat leaf,
Ranunculus

Look to natural
elements, like fire
here, to inspire
both the color
and shape of
an arrangement.

Transitional
From peach to rust

Dahlia,
Ranunculus,
Grapes, Zinnia,
Amaranth, Celosia,
Wax flower,
Pomegranate,
Palm nut

To create the
most painterly
arrangements,
go for a strong
cascade of
elements flowing
out from a vessel.

Accent Color
White with
red accent

Rose, Ranunculus,
Pampas grass

Red is an incredibly
stimulating color.
When used as an
accent, especially
contrasting white
or cool colors,
it energizes
your composition.

Complementary
Rust and
chartreuse

Garden cosmos,
Snake allium, Palm
nut, Grass

Look to the shape
of the vase itself
for inspiration.
The sinuous lines
of florals mimic
the vessel's
curves, resulting
in a coordinated
composition.

Analogous
Beige, pink,
and scarlet

Tulip, Carnation,
Sweet pea,
Bleeding heart,
Rose

Break away from
using roses as the
centerpiece of
an arrangement.
Bleeding hearts can
inspire romance,
creating soft
falling movements
throughout a design.

Accent Color
Pink, orange,
and red with
hot pink accent

Peony, Crown
imperial fritillary,
Tulip, Ranunculus,
Bleeding heart,
Lady's slipper
orchid, Rose

Crown imperial
fritillary can act
as both a face
flower and gestural
element, bringing
movement and a
focal point to
the arrangement.

Accent Color
White with
fuchsia accent

Rose, Daffodil,
Dragon fruit, Sweet
pea, Ranunculus,
Phalaenopsis orchid

Look for produce
with unexpected
patterns. Here, the
inside of the dragon
fruit complements
the color palette of
the florals, uniting
the composition.

Accent Color
Fuchsia and pink
with yellow accent

Peony, Torch ginger,
Ranunculus, Sweet
pea, Pepperberry

Accenting a
stimulating color,
like fuchsia, with
another stimulating
color, like yellow,
heightens the
overall energy
and impact.

Triadic
Golden yellow, pale
blue, and fuchsia

Rose, Ranunculus,
Tweedia, Oncidium
orchid, Sweet pea,
Carnation

Placing florals in
glass cloches
adds texture and
an extra layer
to a composition.
It creates a
contained wildness.

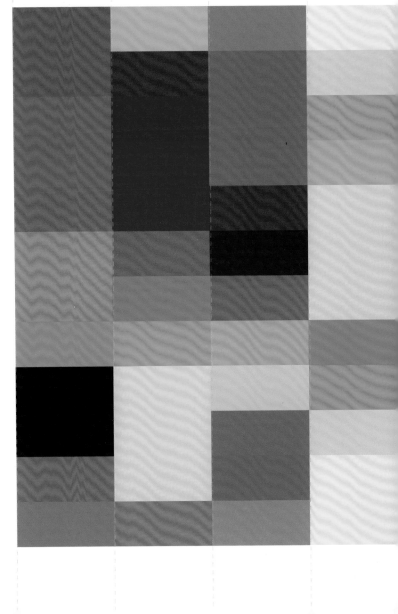

Accent Color
Peach, pink, and
fuchsia with pale
blue accent

Torch ginger,
Phalaenopsis
orchid, Heliconia,
Anthurium, Tweedia,
Pepperberry,
Sweet pea

When designing
with a warm
palette, you can
incorporate a
dash of blue as an
accent color. Here,
appearing as an
upward diagonal,
it creates a
thoughtful break in
the arrangement.

Complementary
Rust and pale blue

Rose, Dried palm
husk, Tweedia,
Thistle, Dried grass,
Cymbidium orchid

As seen here
with the use of
palm husk and
dried grass, highly
graphic elements
can easily generate
an arrangement.
Bold lines make a
strong statement.

Analogous
Peach, pink,
and red

Phalaenopsis
orchid, Heliconia,
Sweet pea, Croton
leaf, Dried branch

When you
lack gestural
elements, include
perpendicular
branches or foliage
to increase height.

Accent Color
Brown, sienna,
and pink with
black accent

Peony, Scabiosa,
Chocolate cosmos,
Rose hip, Burning
bush, Carnation,
Privet berry

Negative space
creates movement
and energy within
an arrangement.
Give gestural
elements room to
breathe by avoiding
overcrowding.

Accent Color
Pink and burgundy
with brown accent

Poinsettia,
Philodendron,
Japanese quince,
Carnation, Teasel,
Eucalyptus, Tomato,
Passion fruit,
Anthurium

Flowers do not
always need to be
at the center of
an arrangement.
Here, tomatoes
and other produce
act as a focal point
from which to
radiate out.

Analogous
Hot pink, burgundy,
and red

Rose, Blood orange,
Peach blossom,
Amaranth,
Variegated Indian
shot leaf, Magnolia
buds, Strawflower,
Calathea leaf

There is always
color inspiration
inside of fruit, like
the vivid burgundy
and red of the
blood orange here.

Analogous
Plum, magenta,
and pink

Peony, Rose,
Bleeding heart,
Sweet pea,
Persian fritillary

Add large,
attention-grabbing
florals, like pink
peonies, to create
a linear visual break
and a balanced
asymmetry.

Accent Color
White and
green with
burgundy accent

Phalaenopsis
orchid, Dahlia,
Camellia leaf

The center of
phalaenopsis
orchids is often
a striking color
like burgundy or
yellow. Use this
characteristic to
pull other florals of
a similar shade into
the arrangement.

Monochromatic
Magenta

Magnolia, Plum blossom

When working with only two flower types, asymmetry results in a noteworthy design.

Accent Color
Magenta with pale blue accent

Bromeliad, Tweedia

Opposites attracting is the key to contrasting soft and sharp, as seen here with the tweedia's soft blooms and the bromeliad's sharp edges.

Analogous
Fuchsia, pink, and amethyst

Anthurium, Peony, Cymbidium orchid, Ranunculus, Pepperberry, Dried branch

Clusters of berries, such as pepperberries, add texture and can unite vessels into a cohesive composition.

Analogous
Pink, fuchsia, purple, and blue

Sweet pea, Dahlia, Tulip, Lisianthus, Delphinium, Coralberry

Having flower faces, such as the tulips here, mirror or "look" at one another creates compositional depth and movement.

Accent Color
Red and
burgundy with pale
blue accent

Rose, Sweet pea,
Garden cosmos,
Palm nut

The cool pale
blue is a strikingly
polar yet appealing
contrast to
the warm red
and burgundy.

Monochromatic
Red

Rose, Amaranth,
Pomegranate

Red can be
interpreted very
subjectively and
can appear dark
and moody in an
arrangement. By
exploring the shape
of the arrangement,
it becomes more
sultry than doleful.

Analogous
Blush, pink, rust,
and burgundy

Rose, Garden
cosmos,
Ranunculus,
Hellebore, Palm
nut, Velvet bush

By not grouping
colors together,
you create
movement within
a composition
made of multiples
of the same vessel.

Complementary
Red and green

Rose, Pitcher plant,
Lady's slipper
orchid, Shelf
mushroom, String
of pearls, Cork oak
bark, Gold dust
dracaena leaf,
New Zealand flax
leaf, Fern

Use variations
of green and red
to dissociate the
familiar color
combination from
the winter holidays.

Transitional
From burgundy
to cream

Amaryllis,
Ranunculus,
Rose, Amaranth,
Sweet pea, Juniper,
Wax flower,
Cotoneaster berry,
Pomegranate

Draping amaranth
around the entirety
of an arrangement
brings all the
elements together
and elicits an
ethereal feel.

Transitional
From fuchsia
to purple

Dahlia,
Philodendron,
Sweet pea,
Ranunculus,
Tulip, Eucalyptus,
Coralberry

Pair fuchsia
with rich jewel
tones for a lavish
arrangement.

Monochromatic
Fuchsia

Dahlia, Lisianthus,
Sweet pea,
Ranunculus,
Coralberry

To achieve a vivid
appearance, vary
stem lengths and
create layers with
the florals.

Accent Color
Brown with
magenta accent

Anemone,
Pitcher plant,
Teasel, Beech,
Andromeda bud

Bring the seasons
indoors with your
floral selections.
Brown and jewel
tones are widely
available during
the autumn
months and mirror
the changing of
the leaves.

Analogous
Dusty rose,
lavender, purple,
and mauve

Rose, Anemone,
Fringed lavender,
Sweet pea,
Thunberg spirea,
Hellebore

Anemone is an
ideal face flower.
Its center is very
defined, offering
a moment of focus.

Accent Color
Lavender and white
with black accent

Scabiosa, Sweet
pea, Hellebore,
Snake's head
fritillary

Embrace subtle
gestures. The
overall shape
here mimics the
soft gestural
tendrils of the
sweet pea, which
were the initial
inspiration for
the arrangement.

Analogous
Lavender,
pale blue, and
silver green

Anemone,
Hyacinth, Palm

When designing
an arrangement,
consider where it
will be displayed.
In entryways or
on console tables,
the addition of
palm or another
leaf to flowers can
create excitement,
whereas the same
inclusion would
not be successful
on a dining table
due to its height.

Monochromatic
Blue

Larkspur, Thistle,
Olive

This arrangement's
lack of face flowers
creates a soft
look, with greater
emphasis on texture
and gesture.

Accent Color
White, cream,
and lavender
with lilac accent

Magnolia, Sweet
pea, Tulip,
Ranunculus,
Daffodil, Lupine,
Lilac, Snake's
head fritillary

Incorporate
accents that
bring both color
and texture to an
arrangement, as
the lilac does here,
adding softness.

Accent Color
Pale blue and
beige with
magenta accent

Magnolia, Larkspur,
Hellebore, Rose,
Lilac, Thunberg
spirea

Add larger florals
to the top of the
arrangement for
an appearance
reminiscent of
a Flemish still life.

Analogous
Plum, mauve,
and cream

Magnolia, Persian
fritillary, Hellebore,
Lilac, Naples onion,
Eucalyptus

Incorporate striking
contrasts in color,
texture, and shape.
The juxtaposition
between the
magnolia and dark
foliage creates
dimensionality.

Accent Color
Lavender, blush,
cream, and
pale blue with
black accent

Ranunculus,
Sweet pea, Tulip,
Rose, Lisianthus,
Larkspur, Scabiosa,
Blackberry,
Privet berry

A black accent adds
a contemporary
edge to soft pastels.

Accent Color
Plum, peach,
and mauve with
apricot accent

Magnolia, Rose,
Ranunculus,
Persian fritillary,
Fox's grape
fritillary, Orchid,
Daffodil

Incorporate
contrasting
shapes into an
arrangement
for a dynamic
presentation.
For instance,
the sharp points
of orchid petals
here juxtapose
and balance the
roundness of
magnolia flowers.

Accent Color
Yellow orange
and peach with
lavender accent

Tulip, Torch ginger,
Ranunculus, Lilac,
Grapefruit, White
jasmine, Pussy
willow, Dutch iris,
Lemon, Willow

The rich citrus
palette of yellow
orange and peach
is extended by
adding grapefruit
and lemons.

Analogous
Apricot, peach,
pink, lavender,
and purple

Torch ginger, Tulip,
Hellebore, Rose,
Heather, Bromeliad,
Sweet pea

The eye-popping
shape of the torch
ginger becomes
the focal point
here and the
arrangement's
face flower.

Analogous
Lavender, lilac,
and mauve

Lilac, Lupine,
Lisianthus, Tulip,
Sweet pea,
Corkscrew hazel

The tightness
of this design is
broken up by the
gestural branches
weaving through
the florals and
thereby creating
movement.

Accent Color
Purple, lavender,
and yellow orange
with peach accent

Tulip, Lisianthus,
Rose, Ranunculus,
Heliconia, Privet
berry, Larkspur,
Fringed lavender

Accent colors
used outside of
an arrangement,
deliberately placed
among the vases,
direct the eye to
view the entirety
of the design.

Triadic
Orange, lavender,
and green

Tulip, Banana,
Heliconia, Papaya,
Sugarcane,
Bromeliad, Lilac,
Sweet pea, Rose,
Persimmon, Ground
cherry

Incorporating
tropical elements,
like sugarcane and
banana, increases
graphic contrast
and texture.

Analogous
Mauve, brown,
and cream

Hellebore,
Corkscrew hazel,
Toyon berry

Featuring
corkscrew
hazel branches
prominently and
unobstructed
highlights the
power of this
arrangement.

Analogous
Lilac, plum, purple,
and mauve

Hellebore,
Magnolia, Tulip,
Lilac, Snake's head
fritillary, Thunberg
spirea, Begonia, Fig

Dark plums
and blacks are
unexpected colors
to represent spring
but are plentiful
in the produce
harvested at that
time of year. Pair
those colors with
lilac and purple to
soften the overall
appearance.

Analogous
Lavender, lilac,
purple, and plum

Rose, Ranunculus,
Agonis, Vanda
orchid, Plum,
Pepino melon,
Delphinium,
Carnation,
Aster, Phlox

When you hide
the vessel under
the flowers, the
arrangement
almost looks like
a natural growth
in the earth.

Analogous
Brown, burgundy,
and purple

Calla lily, Sweet
pea, Philodendron,
Olive fruit,
Eucalyptus

For a dramatic
design, offset
the balance of an
arrangement with
asymmetry—both
vertically and
horizontally.

Accent Color
Brown, purple,
and mauve with
lavender accent

Dried banana leaf,
Rose, Lisianthus,
Tulip, Dried silver
grass, Flamboyant
tree seed pod,
Privet berry

The brown in dried
elements, such
as the leaves and
seed pods here,
adds patina and
gravitas to an
arrangement
filled with softer
tones of lavender
and mauve.

Accent Color
Black with
pink accent

Peony, Begonia,
Calla lily, Chocolate
cosmos, Agonis,
Privet berry,
Strawflower,
Purple millet

To make a bold
statement, create
a linear swath of
an unexpected
color that
runs through a
monochromatic
arrangement.

354   356   358   360

Accent Color
Dark green and
brown with butter
yellow accent

Ranunculus,
Queen Anne's lace,
Cavolo nero kale,
Philodendron,
Fern, Blackberry,
Passion fruit

Using ferns
throughout here
unifies the two
arrangements
into one design.

Accent Color
Black and oxblood
with gray accent

Ranunculus, Calla
lily, Lisianthus,
Privet berry,
Mushroom,
Scabiosa,
Blackberry

Gray is not a
common color
in flowers, but it
can be found
in mushrooms and
bark. Use these
latter elements
to add a touch
of lightness and
texture to a moody
arrangement.

Monochromatic
Black with mauve
accent

Calla lily, Begonia,
Ranunculus, Agonis,
Chocolate cosmos,
Privet berry

In addition to
flowers, use berries,
grasses, and
decorative leaves to
tie an arrangement
together.

Index of flowers

Index of colors and color schemes

Phaidon Press Limited
2 Cooperage Yard
London E15 2QR

Phaidon Press Inc.
111 Broadway
New York, NY 10006

phaidon.com

First published 2021
Reprinted 2024
© 2021 Taylor Putnam and
Michael Putnam

ISBN 978 1 83866 157 1 (US)
ISBN 978 1 83866 235 6 (UK)
ISBN 978 1 83866 240 0 (signed edition)

A CIP catalogue record for this book
is available from the British Library and
the Library of Congress.

Commissioning Editor: William Norwich
Project Editor: Sarah Massey
Production Controller: Sarah Kramer

Designed by João Mota

The publishers would like to thank
Jamie Compton for his help in
confirming the common names of
the flowers.

Printed in China